Coaching at End of Life

Coaching at
End of Life

Dr. Don Eisenhauer, PCC, and
J. Val Hastings, MCC

Dr. Don Eisenhauer, PCC

Email: don@coachingatendoflife.com
Phone: 1-484-948-1894

J. Val Hastings, MCC

Email: val@coaching4clergy.com
Phone: 1-877-381-2672

Web Site: www.coachingatendoflife.com

ISBN 978-0-9894751-0-5

Table of Contents

Foreword vii

Introduction 1

Chapter One: The Need for End-of-Life Coaches 3

Chapter Two: Our Culture's View of End of Life.................................5

Chapter Three: The Church: Help or Hindrance?................................9

Chapter Four: Dealing with the Losses of Life 17

Chapter Five: I'm Doing Well...25

Chapter Six: Coached, Not Counseled..33

Chapter Seven: Coaching the Dying 37

Chapter Eight: Coaching the Grieving..65

Chapter Nine: Children..95

Chapter Ten: Follow Up. Follow Up. Follow Up. 101

Chapter Eleven: The End-of-Life Coach 111

Appendix A: Case Studies for Coaching at End of Life 125

Appendix B: The Eight Building Blocks of Coaching.......................137

Appendix C: Supporting Building Blocks for Coaching the Dying 167

Appendix D: Supporting Building Blocks for Coaching the Grieving 169

References 171

About the Authors..173

Foreword

As I reflect on this book, there are two years that come to mind—1999 and 2010. In 1999, I began working with my first coach and very quickly realized the benefits of coaching in ministry. Working with a coach, I felt empowered and encouraged. People noticed a change in me and commented that I seemed to be at the top of my game. Forward progress was happening on a regular basis. I remember thinking to myself, "What if I adopted a coaching approach to ministry? What if the larger church adopted a coaching approach to ministry?"

In that moment a vision began to emerge—a global vision: every pastor, ministry staff and church leader a coach.

That is our vision at Coaching4Clergy, where we believe that those nine simple words have the ability to radically transform the local church and its leaders. We see this as the next great awakening in Christianity. Picture it … every leader in the church empowering and bringing out the best in others:

- Pastors and leaders at their best,

- Teams and groups making progress,

- Each person in the church effectively contributing in their area,

- Life change happening in our life groups and study groups,

- Visitors feeling empowered, never judged, and

- Pastoral care that is healthy and really helpful.

The second year that comes to mind with the writing of this book is 2010. That's the year that my longtime college friend, Don Eisenhauer, attended his first coach training event. I could tell by the expression on Don's face that the coaching skills he was learning and seeing demonstrated were having a significant impact on him, both personally and professionally.

Don quickly began weaving his new found coaching skills with his years of experience as a pastor, counselor and hospice chaplain. Our regular breakfast meetings at Shorty's for baked oatmeal were the setting for much of the discussion and planning for this book and training materials. The additional Building Blocks that Don offers for coaching the dying and coaching the grieving are a perfect complement to the Core Coaching Competencies. The end result is an entirely new approach to coaching the dying and the grieving.

In this book, Don and I have combined our expertise to offer you a new approach to this topic. We have intentionally divided our writing contributions. Don contributing the first section, while my contribution is primarily the forward and appendix. This was done to insure that those reading this book develop awareness and expertise in both arenas: coaching, as well as end of life. It is my belief that this book will have a positive impact on a coach-approach to ministry, especially the care that we, as pastors, chaplains, hospice workers and volunteers, offer the dying and grieving. Thank you, Don.

Enjoy the book!

Val

Introduction

T he routine is pretty much the same every morning. I wake up, make my coffee, feed the dog, prepare my breakfast, and open the local paper to the obituary page. I am not looking to see if my name is there. Rather, as one who spends most of his time dealing with end-of-life issues—caring for the dying and the grieving—I am checking out the "status" of my parishioners.

What amazes me is that almost every morning the obituary section of my local paper is full. People die every single day—rich people and poor people; those with large families and those who are totally alone; those whose death was long and drawn out and those whose death was sudden and tragic. I can't help but reflect on what their death might have been like. Was it a peaceful death with dignity? Were they prepared for eternity? Did the dying have support to face the final chapter of their life? Did they take advantage of the opportunities that this time brings?

Along with the names of the deceased is a list of the survivors who are left to grieve the loss of their loved one. I look to see if there will be a funeral service and, if so, who will conduct it. I wonder who will support these individuals in their grief. Are they connected to a church or parish or synagogue where they have available spiritual support? If so, are the spiritual leaders prepared and equipped to do so effectively?

In my years of ministry, I have found no greater privilege than to walk a dying person to the door of eternity, then to support their loved ones in the sometimes dark and lonely tunnel of grief that follows.

I have a passion to care for and to support those who are facing these end-of-life issues. Recently, however, my passion has shifted to teaching and supporting the clergy and other professionals who care for people in this difficult time that is filled with so many opportunities and possibilities.

My passion stems from an awareness that, in my 15 years of pastoral ministry, there is so much more I could have done to care for the dying and the grieving. I did the very best that I knew how. Having spent a dozen years as a hospice chaplain and grief care specialist, I now realize that my sincere attempts at ministering to these individuals were not always the best or most effective. I also see and talk with other clergy who are struggling in the same way I did, whether they realize it or not.

Please understand, this textbook is not meant to be an exhaustive study on the topic of death and dying. Nor is it meant to be a comprehensive study of grief and loss. There are already excellent books available on these subjects. The purpose of this textbook is to help guide and instruct every pastor, ministry staff and church leader in using coaching principles as a methodology in ministering to those who are dying or grieving.

Thank you for caring enough about those you serve to embark on this training.

The opportunities ahead are endless.

NOTE: For an understanding of why there is a picture of a dragonfly on the front cover of this book and how dragonflies remind us of end-of-life care, go to www.coachingatendoflife.com and download the free eBook "Life Lessons from Dragonflies."

Chapter One

The Need for End-of-Life Coaches

"I help people get the results they want by bringing out the best in them." This is the way J. Val Hastings, founder of Coaching4Clergy, defines what a coach does. "I also explain that coaching isn't about fixing people or solving problems; coaching is a developmental or discovery-based process. Similar to athletic coaches, we further develop the skill and talent already inherent in the people we coach" (Hastings 2010, 5).

I am convinced that, in most cases, people have within them everything they need to deal with the inevitable "end-of-life" issues which every human being must face. For many reasons, however, most are not aware of how to tap into those resources. In addition, many feel inadequate and embarrassed, thinking they are not handling the issues well and fearing they are not "normal."

What these individuals need is an end-of-life coach. This is a person who will partner with both the dying and the grieving (Hastings 2010, 6). This partnership will be focused 100% on the person being coached, and will build a safe and trusting relationship where anything and everything can be shared. This is so important when dealing with end-of-life issues.

The end-of-life coach will accelerate what is already underway in the coachee (Hastings 2010, 6). In most cases, the individual approaching the end of his or her life, as well as the individual grieving the loss of a loved one, does not need to be fixed! They simply need someone to come alongside of them, someone who, through deep listening and powerful questions, will help them to embrace all that is happening in and around them, and to seek God's transformation in the midst of it.

This last statement captures Val's third component involved in the definition of a coach, namely, that the end-of-life coach will maximize potential, moving people from good to great. Here the "great" can mean a good, peaceful death, or it can mean healthy grief and mourning. Most of the time, we have no choice as to whether or not we will deal with end-of-life issues as a part of our daily life. Doing so is inevitable, whether we want to or not! But we do have a choice as to whether our death, or the death of a loved one, will be a good and peaceful death. We also have a choice as to whether our time of grieving and mourning will be healthy and a time of growth. The problem is most of us cannot bring this about on our own. We need someone to come alongside of us and help bring out the potential within. When we feel like we are going crazy, we need to be reminded that we are normal. When we feel so alone, we need to be supported. When it seems too difficult to go on, we need to be encouraged. When our story begs to be told, we need someone to listen. And when we feel hopeless and want to give up, we need someone to help in the forming of a new vision for the future.

This is the role of the end-of-life coach. In our day and age, the end-of-life coach is desperately needed. We need end-of-life coaches in our churches and parishes and synagogues. We need them in our community and parachurch organizations. Wherever we have people—people who deal with grief and loss (which is everyone!)—we need end-of-life coaches!

Chapter Two

Our Culture's View of End of Life

We live in a culture that does not deal well with end-of-life issues. This is true for the process of dying as well as the process of grieving. People don't like to talk about death. For many, the subject is taboo. If the topic is brought up, some will change the subject, while others will walk away. It makes many people uncomfortable. For some people, the underlying assumption is that if I talk about death, it might happen to me. So, I am not going to even mention it.

As a result of this underlying assumption, we have come up with many euphemisms related to dying and death. There are literally hundreds of euphemisms for death in the English language. Instead of saying someone has died, we say they expired, or passed away, or kicked the bucket. They bit the big one, or croaked, or have given up the ghost. We refer to a dead person as being six feet under, or say they are pushing up daisies. We say they cashed in their chips, or checked out. They danced the last dance and have bought the farm. All this and much, much more, all because we don't like to mention the word "dead."

While some purposely don't talk about end-of-life issues, I get the sense that for other Americans, we have been so conditioned by our culture that we fail to accept that death is inevitable. North America is the only continent that acts as if death is optional.

Think about it. There are many physicians that seldom discuss life's final stage. They continue to offer treatments to their patients, even when they are of little or no benefit.

When a person has a loved one who dies, they are faced with the reality of death. Yet those around them may still refuse to acknowledge this reality. The mourner has to be back to work in three days. Some will never mention a word about his or her loss. Others will make comments such as, "It's been a month, aren't you over it yet?!" In other words, they are saying, "You are making me uncomfortable! Please don't talk about it! Please don't make me face this reality!"

We treat death far more as an enemy to be fought, rather than an experience to be embraced and befriended.

Another place in our culture where I see this being lived out is in the funeral business. In the years that I have been serving as a hospice chaplain, I have noticed quite a shift in the way that people respond following the death of their loved one. It used to be common practice for there to be a viewing, and then a funeral service, and then a burial. Others chose the route of cremation, followed by a memorial service. These were often followed by a funeral or memorial luncheon, where the mourners could gather and find support. Each of these is a wonderful way to grieve and to begin the mourning process. However, times have now changed. Many families are no longer having viewings or funerals or memorial services. More and more people have their loved one cremated, and that is the end—no ceremony, no ritual and no outward expression of mourning. One funeral director told me that he has seen a trend of families who never return to pick up their loved ones remains after cremation. This is in spite of his continual reminders.

For some, this change in funeral practices has come about because of financial reasons. They don't have the money to pay for a full funeral service. But more times than not, I am finding that the reasons extend to the issues I discuss. People don't want to deal with the end-of-life issue. They want to downplay it or even ignore it as much as possible. They want to move on in life with no interruptions caused by their loved one's death.

I am really concerned about what our culture will be like if this trend continues. Death is not optional! End-of-life issues are a reality. Refusing to deal with this reality does not make it go away. It makes it worse.

On other continents and in earlier centuries here, perspectives were different. The Victorian Era was known for many things, including its views of death. Compared to modern attitudes, our forebears of this era could be accused of having a morbid fascination and peculiar obsession with death and dying. Elaborate rituals surrounded the everyday occurrences of dying and grieving.

The Victorian age was named for England's Queen Victoria. She took the throne in 1837 and died in 1901. Victoria's husband, Prince Albert, died of typhoid in 1861. During this period of forty years, the Queen was in mourning. She remained in full mourning for three years and dressed her entire court in mourning attire.

The Victorian Era reflected the Queen's personal attitude toward mourning. The longest mourning period was for the death of a spouse and usually lasted a minimum of two years. But just grieving was not enough; a person was required to dress for the occasion. There were even stages of mourning, requiring different apparel. Full mourning lasted a year and one day, and women were expected to wear black crepe or dull materials that had no sheen or shine. Black was the preferred color because it symbolized the absence of light and life. Special mourning lace handkerchiefs had black borders. For the head, there were special bonnets, caps and veils for grieving women. During crying fits, the large cuffs on the dresses would be used to wipe the nose; they were referred to as "weepers."

For one entire year, a woman could not leave her house without full mourning attire and a weeping veil. She could attend church services, but was never to be seen at places of amusement or entertainment. Even the houses were fully draped in black crepe banners to signify that there had been a death. At the moment of death, clocks would be stopped, curtains drawn over the windows, and mirrors covered.

Men had it much easier during times of grief. They had a shorter mourning period and simpler clothes. Some men wore full black suits, but most men just wore a black hat band and a black arm band.

As time went on, America's mourning traditions were changed out of necessity, as we engaged in various wars. With so many men on the battlefield, women were forced into the workplace and could no longer abide by the restrictions that the elaborate grief process required.

I am thankful that we no longer have to observe such restrictive rituals as part of our mourning, yet our society today can learn some valuable lessons from the Victorian grieving practices. The Victorian Era allowed the grieving person to acknowledge their loss publicly and to talk about it openly. Much more time was allowed to mourn a close loved one in those days, as death was not a taboo subject.

We have come so far from those Victorian times. Our culture has swung completely in the opposite direction. Those who care for the dying and the grieving must be aware of the culture in which we live, and of the subtle and not so subtle messages that are being proclaimed daily about end-of-life issues. These messages must be addressed!

Chapter Three

The Church: Help or Hindrance?

I lift up my eyes to the hills. Where does my help come from? My help comes from the Lord, the maker of heaven and earth. —Psalm 121:1

When an individual is facing end-of-life issues—either they or a loved one is dying, or someone has died, and they are grieving—where should they turn for help? Should they not turn to their church, where they can find the Lord's help?

The answer to that question should be YES! There should be no greater or more helpful place to find help when dealing with end-of-life issues. However, my experience shows that what "should" be is not always the case. As a matter of fact, I would go as far as to say that more often than not, I see and hear stories of the church being more of a hindrance than a help in these end-of-life matters. It saddens me greatly, because it need not be that way.

How can the church end up being more of a hindrance than a help? Consider some thoughts:

1. Cultural Principles Permeate the Church

In the last chapter, we talked about the culture in which we live. It is a culture that does not want to deal with end-of-life issues. Many don't like to talk about it. They avoid the topic at any cost and, in the process, avoid the individuals who are in the midst of an end-of-life crisis.

Since the church is made up of people—people who are part of the current culture—it becomes easy for those same feelings and responses to become part of the church. Those who are struggling with a life-threatening illness and those who are grieving the loss of a loved one will sometimes feel just as isolated and alone as those who are not a part of a church. Why? Often the church culture is not any different. In many cases, it is even more difficult for churchgoers, because they expect it to be different. They expect their church family to support them, and are devastated when they don't.

2. The Clergy Don't Know Any Better

It is not only the parishioners who bring into the church our current cultural ideas concerning end-of-life issues. The clergy often do the same. It's not that they want to be this way, but they truly do not know any better. They were never taught.

I think back to my own story. I had a wonderful seminary experience, which prepared me well for pastoral ministry. I remember one lecture in my Pastoral Counseling class dealing with grief and loss, and I remember one class in my Preaching Course dealing with funerals. That, however, was the extent of my training on end-of-life issues. I am not blaming my seminary. There is only so much material that can fit into a three-year program. I am just trying to point out the reality. What made all of this worse is that I had no clue how little I knew. I thought I was well prepared to minister to people who were dealing with end-of-life issues. Yet I look back now on my early years of ministry, and I realize that in many cases I was more of a hindrance than a help. That makes me sad. But that is one of the reasons why I am writing this book. My own story has made me passionate about helping other clergy to minister in end-of-life issues.

Another major issue for clergy is lack of time. Clergy are stretched thin and simply do not have the time to give extensive care. Bereaved parishioners feel isolated as the pastor moves on to the next family crisis. (See Chapter 10 and information on the Bereavement Management System software as a solution for this issue.)

3. Typical Godly Response

When you take a group from a faith community, who truly care for one another, and add to that people whose primary training on end-of-life issues is from our current culture, you get the following:

When it comes to someone who is dying or has been diagnosed with a life-threatening illness, the most common response by both clergy and lay people is avoidance. When I question clergy about why they are not visiting their dying parishioners, the response I typically get is that they push it off because they feel so uncomfortable and inadequate. They don't know what to do or what to say, or they don't know how to bring comfort in the situation, or they don't know how to explain what is happening to their parishioners, or it makes them feel so uncomfortable that they avoid ministering as they know they should. If this were the exception, I wouldn't even mention it. But I find it to be much more the rule rather than the exception. And whether they tell their clergy or not, their dying parishioners are crushed by their lack of presence and response.

When it comes to caring for the grieving, the response is usually very different. Rather than avoidance, the problem I typically see in the church is that the members and clergy care too much. They are too nice! How can one care too much or be too nice? We will cover this in more detail in the coming chapters, but when a person experiences a loss, the most important thing for them to do is to mourn that loss. The church becomes a hindrance when they care so much about making the individual feel comfortable that they don't allow them to mourn. They don't want their friend or parishioner to hurt or feel bad. This is admirable. But it doesn't allow the grieving to grieve.

4. Fear

Sometimes the issue is fear:

- I am afraid they will ask me something I cannot do or cannot answer.

- I am afraid of what to say. I don't want to make it worse.

- I don't want to evoke strong feelings.

- What if they die while I am there?

- I was taught how to do, not how to be or what to say to individuals and families who are dealing with end-of-life issues.

- If I ask an open-ended question, I don't know where the conversation will go. I am afraid to make them cry.

- I am afraid it will make me cry. I am so sensitive.

5. Misuse of Scripture or Bad Theology

To say that Christians ought not to grieve, or that they should not get depressed when they are told they have a life-threatening illness, is ridiculous. This is cruel and amounts to telling them to "get over it." Yet well meaning people (lay and clergy alike) say those words over and over again: "If you mourn, or shed tears, or get scared, or show excessive emotions, or question 'why?,' you are showing a lack of faith and are not trusting God. That's what the Bible says!" The Bible states, "We don't want you to ... grieve like the rest of men, who have no hope." (1 Thess. 4:13). Whether those words are spoken, or just implied by people's behaviors, I understand why some people avoid going to church while experiencing end-of-life issues. They find churches to be a hindrance rather than a help.

Working through all the emotions of dying, and experiencing grief and mourning, are in no way a sign of being an immature Christian, or a person who lacks faith. The Apostle

Paul does say that we should not grieve as those who have no hope—but he never says "Don't grieve!" Paul is expressing that true, godly grief, as real as it is, should be tempered by the unshakable hope grounded in the resurrection of the Savior, Jesus Christ.

Both the dying and the grieving experience a whole range of emotions that are normal. Look to the Old Testament to see how Job experienced and worked through his spectrum of emotions. He was numb as he encountered one loss after another, losing everything that he considered precious. He was angry when his wife told him to curse God and die. He was probably frightened as his illnesses continued to worsen. He was upset that he could not seem to die. He was at first glad and then sad when his three friends showed up to comfort him and, as they continued to "comfort" him, he grew increasingly lonely because they proved to be no comfort at all. He wanted them to leave! That is all normal grief—not an expression of a lack of faith.

Acts 8:2 says, "Godly men buried Stephen and mourned deeply for him." This fits right into the Apostle Paul's directive to the Romans to "mourn with those who mourn" (Romans 2:15). The elders of the Ephesian church reacted in this way when Paul left them: "They all wept … What grieved them most was his statement that they would never see his face again " (Acts 20:37-38).

Scripture has numerous examples of intense grief. Abraham and Isaac mourned the loss of Sarah (Gen. 23:2; 24:67). The Israelites grieved the death of Jacob (Gen. 50:10), Aaron (Num. 20:29), Moses (Deut. 34:8), Samuel (1 Sam. 28:3), Saul and Jonathan (2 Sam. 1:12, 17), Josiah (2 Chron. 35:25), along with many others. In the New Testament, Jesus withdrew privately to grieve the death of John the Baptist (Matt. 14:13). He openly wept in grief and in empathy with his friends, Mary and Martha, at the tomb of their brother, Lazarus (John 11:35). Devout believers mourned the death of the deacon Stephen (Acts 8:2). Godly women wept openly for the loss of Tabitha in Joppa (Acts 9:39).

All this, and yet some well meaning pastors and church members say it is inappropriate to grieve openly, and that it shows a lack of faith. No wonder some who are dying or grieving stay away from the church, saying it is more of a hindrance than a help!

6. The Use of Clichés—Religious & Secular

As I spend time listening to the dying and the grieving, one of the biggest frustrations I hear concerns the comments that others make to them. Many are uncomfortable with silence and, when they talk with someone facing end-of-life issues, they feel the need to say something. Not knowing what to say, they frequently put their foot in their mouth and say things that are hurtful, and sometimes even harmful, to the one they are trying to console. The church is no exception to this. As a matter of fact, it is one of the most common places people are faced with these clichés – usually, in this setting, the religious ones. Sadly, the religious clichés are the most devastating. There is no easy way to respond to them.

This is such a common frustration and a major hindrance to the help and healing of the dying and the grieving, a separate book could easily be written on just this topic. For the sake of brevity, however, allow me to share some of the most popular clichés I hear—both religious and secular—which definitely are a hindrance to those at end-of-life:

- Death happens. Get over it.

- Life goes on.

- Count your blessings.

- It was God's will.

- You are still young. You can have another child/marry again.

- There are other fish in the sea.

- God only takes the best and the brightest.

- Be grateful you had him for as long as you did.

- He's in a better place now.

- Something must have been wrong already.

- You are better off.

- Keep your chin up.

- God doesn't give you anything you can't handle.

- Be thankful you have another daughter.

- You have to get on with your life.

- There is a reason for everything.

- You have your whole life ahead of you.

- Just think of all you have to be thankful for.

- I know how you feel.

- You should be glad he/she is out of pain.

- There are other people in much worse situations.

- Time will heal.

- She was so good, God wanted her with Him.

- God called you to this ministry.

- At least you didn't have time to get attached to your baby.

- She brought this on herself.

- Try not to cry. He or she wouldn't want you to cry.

- It's time to put this behind you.

- Aren't you over him yet? He has been dead for awhile now.

- It could have been worse.

- If you think this is bad, I know a family ...

- This isn't nearly as bad as when my mother died.

- It must be a relief.

7. The Need to Defend God

I will mention here one final reason that the church can end up being more of a hindrance than a help when it comes to end-of-life issues. That is, when religious people feel the need to defend God.

Facing end-of-life issues is never fun, and it is almost never one's choice to go through it. As a matter of fact, most people pray that they will be spared from going through it! The problem comes when this prayer is not answered, or at least not answered the way they want.

Following the news that one has a terminal illness, or following the death of a loved one, the most often asked question is "Why?" Why am I the one to get cancer? Why did God take my loved one? Why didn't He answer my prayer and heal him?

Many get angry at God. "How could a loving God do this?"

Some wonder if God is punishing them for some sin they have committed. They are upset because God has rejected them, and they don't understand why.

Some, like Job, will curse God!

I could go on and on ...

All of the above are normal reactions following the news that one is dying, or following the death of a loved one. Their anger is taken out on God. Telling these people that they are out of line with their comments, or trying to defend God is not the most helpful response. For one, God does not need to be defended. But even more, standing up for God is not what will help draw the hurting individual closer to God (which is usually the church member's intent). When the church feels the need to defend God in these situations, the result is usually to push the person away from God. Those who defend God to the dying and the grieving end up being far more of a hindrance than a help.

Chapter Four

Dealing with the Losses of Life

Throughout this textbook, my focus is on coaching individuals who are dealing with end-of-life issues—namely that they are dying, or that their loved ones are dying or have died.

The principles learned here, however, are applicable to coaching those who are dealing with all of the losses of life.

Loss is one of our constant companions throughout life. For many, LOSS is truly a four-letter word—it is a curse word, not to be mentioned. But for most of us, it is almost always there. Each one of us faces issues of loss all the time.

From the moment we are conceived, our lives are a series of transitions:

- We slide from the dark, cozy womb into the bright, cold world—a shocking transition indeed.

- We nurse at the breast and then we are weaned.

- We attach to our parents, and then are forced to detach from them when we are placed in day care or preschool.

- Our baby teeth fall out.

- We make friends and lose them.

- Our parents may divorce.

- Someone we love may die.

- We sometimes move to a new neighborhood.

- We leave home to go to school.

- A pet dies.

- A best friend moves away.

- A boyfriend or girlfriend decides they no longer love us.

- We get a job, and we lose it.

- A person we love dies.

- The time comes when we are told that we are dying.

(Adapted from *Living in the Shadow of the Ghosts of Grief,* Wolfelt 2007, pp. 13-14.)

We could go on and on … Life is filled with transitions and losses.

Nobody likes to lose. Life is supposed to be filled with winners. Look at the headlines on the sports pages.

Losing hurts. It causes pain. It hurts even more because we haven't been taught to expect loss as a part of life, nor have we been taught how to handle the losses of life.

We want to be winners. We want success. We want to be in control of our lives, so we build walls around us with signs that say, "Losses—No Trespassing!" Then if they occur, we feel violated. We say something is wrong. We get angry with God. But the problem is, they keep occurring. We can't get away from them.

We have good reason to not like loss. Too often, a person who has suffered a loss is blamed for it:

- She must not have been a good wife for him to leave her.

- They failed as parents. Otherwise, that child would have stayed in the church and wouldn't have become involved with that crowd.

- He lost his job. I wonder what he did wrong.

- If they had been living a Godly life, this wouldn't have happened.

People in Jesus' day had the same thoughts. In John 9:1-3, we're told:

> As Jesus went along, he saw a man blind from birth. His disciples asked him, "Rabbi, who sinned, this man or his parents, that he was born blind?" "Neither this man nor his parents sinned," said Jesus, "but this happened so that the works of God might be displayed in him.

Losses are a part of life. Ecclesiastes 3:1-4 states:

> There is a time for everything, and a season for every activity under the heavens: a time to be born and a time to die, a time to plant and a time to uproot, a time to kill and a time to heal, a time to tear down and a time to build, a time to weep and a time to laugh, a time to mourn and a time to dance.

Not only are losses a part of life, but losses come in all shapes and sizes.

Some losses are over in 24 hours. Others last for years. Others you never get over. How you respond to your losses, or what you let them do to you, will affect you the rest of your life. You can't avoid loss or shrug it off. Loss is going to be a part of our lives, whether we acknowledge those losses or not.

Loss is not the enemy; not facing its existence is. Unfortunately, many of us have become more proficient in developing denial than we are in facing and accepting the losses of life.

The truth of the matter is loss isn't always a bad thing. As a matter of fact, loss can be good! With each loss comes the potential for change, growth, new insights, understanding and refinement—all words of hope. The problem is, they are often in the future, and we are unable to see that far ahead when we are in the midst of our grief.

Life is a blending of loss and gain. Let me give you some examples:

- A bud is lost when it turns into a beautiful rose.

- When a plant pushes its way up through the soil, a seed is lost.

- When you were a child, your baby teeth came in after bouts of pain and crying, but they were lost in order to make room for the permanent teeth. Sometimes these too are lost and replaced by false teeth.

- Graduating from high school produced a loss of status, friends, and familiarity, but most of us looked forward to it, for it meant going on with our lives.

Change usually involves some form of loss of the way things were at one time.

In the New Testament, the Apostle Paul told the Ephesians (4:22-24): "You were taught, with regard to your former way of life, to put off your old self ... and to put on the new self. ... The 'new self' comes as a result of the loss of the 'old self.'"

Some of the losses of life can be obvious: losing a loved one through death or divorce; a car is stolen; a house is vandalized and robbed.

Some are not as obvious: changing jobs, receiving a "B" instead of an "A" in a college course, getting less than we had hoped for in a raise, moving, illness (loss of health), a new teacher in the middle of a semester, a son or daughter going off to school, the loss of a dream or lifetime goal. All of these are losses, but because they may not be easy to recognize, we do not identify them as such. Therefore, we don't spend time and energy dealing with them.

Many of the losses of life are related to aging.

Childhood and adolescent romances are filled with losses—some daily, even hourly! Moving from school to school, failing a grade, dropping out, leaving home for college, moving away from family, even if planned—these changes contain loss.

When you hit the job market, losses multiply as rejections occur. Someone else gets the promotion, deals fall through, businesses fail, the economy falters.

There are physical losses—ironically, a major one involves the gain of pounds and inches! We lose our youth or beauty or smooth skin or muscle tone or our shape.

In the middle years, the losses become more frequent and more negative. Who rejoices over lost hair, teeth, or graduating to bifocals? We don't usually call these growth experiences. Losses seem to build on losses. We tend to lose more friends as the years go on.

Threatened losses are difficult. The possibility of their occurring is real, but there is little you can do about it. Your sense of control is destroyed. You've been working for 19 years at the same company. At 20 years, all of your benefits are secure. Then you are informed that, due to a sluggish economy, 40% of the employees at your company will be terminated at the end of the month, and length of employment is no criteria for being retained. Will you be one of the 40 percent?

There are many other threatened losses in life: waiting for biopsy results; a spouse saying, "I'm thinking of divorcing you"; a romantic interest who doesn't call anymore; a business investment that may not come through; being sued by an angry customer or employee; a friend who tells you he suspects your son has been using drugs for the past year.

All of the above are potential losses. They could occur. There is little you can do about them, and you feel the loss before it occurs—you feel helpless. But they need to be dealt with!

Being part of a church or parish or synagogue brings losses that would not be there otherwise. People leave the church. Sometimes clergy leave. Sometimes there are church splits.

Having a disease such as cancer is considered a major loss because of the health change. But have you considered all of the additional secondary losses? Loss of a familiar home environment, loss of independence, loss of control, a loss of auto-nomy, loss of bodily functions, loss of body parts, loss of predictability, loss of pleasure, loss of identity, loss of intimacy, loss of hope, loss of job, loss of enjoyable hobbies, loss of social interaction or contacts, loss of self-esteem, or loss of mobility.

And each loss needs a grief reaction. Each one needs to be mourned. The meaning and extent of each loss varies for each person, depending on the investment that was made. The amount of grieving varies, but many could benefit from an end-of-life coach who understands these losses!

The death of a significant person is what we usually think of first when we talk about grief or loss, but how about all the secondary losses that go along with that? Loss of hopes, dreams, wishes, fantasies, feelings, expectations, and the needs you had for that person. It's not only what you lose in the present, but what you lose in the future as well.

A widow has not only lost her husband, but has also lost a partner to share retirement, church functions, couples groups, a child's wedding, a grandchild's first birthday, and so on.

Identifying some of the roles that a deceased person played in your life may help you understand the direction your life will now be taking. Think of someone close to you whom you have lost, or think about what it would be like if the person you most share your life with died. Which of the following apply:

Friend, handyperson, lover, gardener, companion, sports partner, checkbook balancer, garbage taker outer, mechanic, encourager, motivator, business partner, errand person, tax preparer, spouse, child, parent, brother, sister, provider, cook, bill payer, laundry person, confidant, mentor, prayer partner, source of inspiration, teacher, counselor, protector, organizer.

Understand?

There are losses that come as a result of divorce. There are losses that come as a result of abandonment—whether physical or emotional abandonment.

These are all common losses. The majority of losses we experience are difficult to grieve over. Why? Because they are not usually recognized as losses. The trouble with trying to mourn loss when death isn't involved is that there is no body, no funeral, and no public shoulder to cry on. There is no traditional, socially sanctioned outlet for mourning when the loss isn't death.

And, you see, losses are cumulative. Past losses have an effect on current losses and attachments. And when we don't deal with the losses of life—when we don't properly grieve them—unresolved reactions and feelings lead to a higher level of discomfort, and these unresolved issues continue to prevent us from living life to the fullest. There are times when we lose hope and remain stuck with pain from the past.

Have you ever caught some flies and imprisoned them in a glass jar with air holes at the top? Some of us did this as children. If you do this, you will notice that the flies buzz around frantically looking for a way out of the jar. But keep the jar closed for several days and something interesting begins to happen. When you take the perforated lid off, the flies don't try to escape. Even though there is no lid, the flies are so used to flying around in a circle, they continue to do so. And even when they get close to the top, they go right back to flying around in a circle.

Well, sometimes people do the same thing. We carry our losses with us like emotional baggage, and even though the lid of the jar has been removed, we continue to fly in circles.

Who taught you how to handle the losses of life? For most of us, probably no one. In our families, we are taught that acquisition, whether material or nonmaterial things, is the way to be happy and satisfied. We learn to be good in order to acquire attention and praise from parents and other adults. In school, the acquisition of grades gives acceptance and approval. Parents rarely teach us how to handle loss, disappointment, and failure.

The drive to acquire continues throughout life. Isn't this what the advertisers tell us is needed to be successful? Thus, we grow up with the myth that "acquiring is normal; loss is abnormal." Loss to us feels wrong and unnatural. How you respond to losses today and tomorrow may be the result of how you responded to the early losses in your life. (See Chapter 11, "The End-of-Life Coach," for some questions to help you evaluate your response to some of the early losses in your life.)

Every loss is important. It is part of life and cannot be avoided. Losses are necessary! You grow by losing and then accepting the loss. Change occurs through loss. Growth occurs through loss. Life can take on a deeper and richer meaning because of losses. The better you handle them, the healthier you will be and the more you will grow. No one said that loss was fair, but it is a part of life.

For people of faith, the issue of loss has additional meaning – spiritual growth. Loss can strengthen our faith. It enables us to trust more in God and His resources than in ourselves.

With every loss, we are reminded of the fact that we are not in control, and we are not self-sufficient. Loss produces maturity. Romans 5:3-4 says:

> Not only so, but we also glory in our sufferings, because we know that suffering produces perseverance; perseverance, character; and character, hope.

Loss reminds us that we cannot always have immediate gratification. We can't always have what we want, when we want it, no matter what.

When you experience a loss, like the Apostle Paul, your beliefs can change. Paul discovered the purpose of losses. In 2 Corinthians 12:1-10, he talked about his thorn in the flesh. He wanted it to leave and it wouldn't. But he learned that there was a purpose for this thorn. God's power would be more evident in his life because of its presence.

When you experience loss, you might discover the extent of the comfort of God. 2 Corinthians 1:3-7 states:

> Praise be to the God and Father of our Lord Jesus Christ, the Father of compassion and the God of all comfort, who comforts us in all our troubles, so that we can comfort those in any trouble with the comfort we ourselves receive from God. For just as we share abundantly in the sufferings of Christ, so also our comfort abounds through Christ. If we are distressed, it is for your comfort and salvation; if we are comforted, it is for your comfort, which produces in you patient endurance of the same sufferings we suffer. And our hope for you is firm, because we know that just as you share in our sufferings, so also you share in our comfort.

Loss can bring people together in a way never experienced before. We are called to comfort each other (1 Thess. 4:18) and to weep with those who weep (Rom. 12:15).

Our losses can change our values. The questions "Why did I spend so much time on that?" and "Why did I waste all those years?" are common when one is grieving over the loss of a loved one. Hopefully we will learn through those experiences to the extent that our lives are different.

The key to all of this is: Our losses must be dealt with! We need to be aware of them! We need to grieve them! As Alan Wolfelt (2007) states, "If you want to live well and love well, you need to mourn well."

But many are unaware of how to do this. An end-of-life coach walks with them through this process.

Chapter Five

I'm Doing Well

Misunderstandings abound in end-of-life issues. Allow me to share a few of them that will affect our ability to coach people in this stage of life.

Let us start with the reality that we are all going to die. As stated earlier, the initial thought that most people have when they think about death is that it is scary. It is horrible. It is the worst thing that could ever happen to anyone. This is a misunderstanding and is not necessarily the case. Although it is unwanted and not what the individual or family would have chosen, the time leading up to a person's death can be poignant, healing and meaningful.

I found this to be true when my father was dying a few years ago. My father and I had a good relationship. Through my high school and college years, we worked in the family business together. When Dad became sick and was placed onto hospice care, I was devastated. I was not ready for him to die. Yet, I can now look back and say that those months leading up to his death were truly the best times we ever spent together. Knowing that he was dying, we both said things that we had never said before. We both did things we had never done before. We grew even closer in those months. I would not be where I am today, and might not be writing this book, were it not for the meaningful time I spent with my dad while he was dying.

My dad experienced what we often refer to in hospice care as a "good death." I see two elements that make a death "good." The first is that the death goes well. The second is that the person who is dying is well when they die.

Let me explain it this way. I regularly teach a class to those who care for the dying, which I've entitled "The Last Chapter." It talks about the things that a dying person (one in the last chapter of their life) needs in order for them to have a "good death." I usually begin my class with the following first person soliloquy:

I never imagined it would be so hard—especially at first. It came as such a shock. It caught me so off guard. I thought I was doing well. I had all kinds of things planned for the future. Places I wanted to go, people I wanted to see, things I wanted to do.

And then I got the news—"You're dying."

Dying? Me? At first I didn't believe it. I thought it had to be a mistake. But it wasn't. It was real. I was dying and there was nothing I could do about it.

You have no idea what it's like. I had no idea what it would be like. I didn't think it would be such a big deal. I thought I would be prepared. I thought I would be ready. But it's like nothing I've ever had to face before.

It hit me that I was entering into the last chapter of my life here on this earth. What would I do? How would I spend my time? How would I prepare? What would the last chapter of my life be like?

Was it going to be painful? Would I even be able to endure the pain? I'm scared about that.

And what will people be like when they find out I have "The Big C"? Will they be afraid to get near me, thinking my cancer is contagious? Will they treat me like some freak? Will they stand by me to the end?

It scares me that they're not telling me the truth about what's going on in my body either. I see people whispering … What are they not telling me? Don't I have a right to know?

I want to know everything—not so I can dwell on it and be depressed, but so that I might know how to make the best use of my time. Give me a say in the decisions that are to be made. Even though my body is dying, I'm still a living human being. Please treat me as such.

I don't want the last chapter of my life to be one filled with pain and regret and loneliness. I don't want it to slip away without me knowing what is going on. I want the last chapter of my life to be rich and fulfilling and rewarding, even while my body declines. I want to live fully until the moment that I die. I am hopeful about what that can mean and what that can be like.

Will you help me to do that? Will you care for me, in ways I can't care for myself? Will you help me hold onto this hope of living fully until I die? Will you support me through the good days and the rough ones, through the times when I'm up and the times when I'm really down?

I want to seek God and make sure I am prepared for whatever lies beyond this life. I want to enter into eternity with confidence and total peace—peace that all has been completed in this life, and that all is ready for my eternity.

I want to die well. I want a death that goes well, but I also want to be a person who is well when I die—well emotionally, relationally, spiritually, and physically, with little pain.

But I know I can't do it alone. Will you help me? Will you help me make this last chapter of my life the very best that it can be? I need you.

From there, I use the soliloquy to go on to talk about the things that a person who is dying needs. The 16 needs, adapted from David Kessler's book, *The Needs of the Dying* (2007), are:

1. The need to be treated as a living human being.
2. The need to maintain a sense of hopefulness, however changing its focus.
3. The need to be cared for by those who can maintain a sense of hopefulness, however changing this may be.
4. The need to express feelings and emotions about death in one's own way.
5. The need to participate in decisions concerning one's care.
6. The need to be cared for by compassionate, sensitive, knowledgeable people.
7. The need for continuing medical care, even though the goals may change from "cure" to "comfort" goals.
8. The need to have all questions answered honestly and fully.
9. The need to seek spirituality.
10. The need to be free of physical pain.
11. The need to express feelings and emotions about pain in one's own way.
12. The need of children to participate in death.
13. The need to understand the process of death.
14. The need to die in peace and dignity.
15. The need not to die alone.
16. The need to know that the sanctity of the body will be respected after death.

When these needs are met, the process of dying can be a wonderful, helpful, meaningful time of growth, even when we would never choose to go through it.

Having explored the misconception that dying is always scary, horrible and the worst thing that can happen to someone, it is important to ask the following question. When I am in the midst of the process of dying, what does it mean that "I am doing well"?

The first response for many would be that "doing well" means that one is quietly, peacefully accepting their fate, and passively waiting to die. As a result of this thinking, some family members will say to me as a hospice chaplain, "Don't tell my loved one that he is dying. I don't want him to know, because I don't want to scare him. He will be far better off if he never knows." At the same time, I will have some dying patients say to me (sometimes the patients in the same family as referenced above!), "I know that I am dying, but please don't tell my family. I don't want them to know. It will be too hard on them and will upset them too much if they find out." Although these individuals are all well meaning, this is not what it means to be doing well when one is dying! This is a misunderstanding!

To do well when one is dying means that both the dying person and the family are actively working through the feelings that are present at end of life. They are openly communicating about them, and they are openly facing and talking about the issues that present themselves at this time. There are wonderful opportunities at end of life. There are relational opportunities, financial opportunities, personal opportunities and spiritual opportunities. Doing well includes discussing and dealing with all these areas.

When it comes to the grieving, the misunderstandings are even greater. This is especially true when it comes to understanding what it means to be "doing well" in the midst of grief. Because we live in a culture that acts like death is optional rather than inescapable, we typically do a poor job of teaching one another how to grieve a loss. As a result, I will often hear a person who has recently had a loved one die say something like, "I am doing well now. I have a smile on my face and I am feeling good. Last week, however, I was not doing well at all. I lost it. I was crying and hurt so badly I could barely function." This is a common theme after a death has occurred. But, this person has it totally backwards. It is "now" that I would question how well they are doing. Last week is when they were truly "doing well"!

Our culture and the church do not get this. It is the opposite of the way we typically think. Crying and outwardly mourning a loss is often a sign of doing well. Holding it all together and keeping the feelings pressed down inside is often a sign of unhealthy grief—of not doing well. The end-of-life coach must understand this.

I'd like to explore 10 of the common myths regarding grief:

Myth #1: Grief and mourning are the same experience.

Grief is what one feels on the inside after a loved one has died. It is the composite of thoughts and feelings about loss that is experienced internally within an individual. Mourning is the outward expression of that grief. It is the external and visible expression of what is experienced on the inside. Some examples of mourning include crying, talking about the deceased person, funeral or memorial services, acknowledging anniversary dates, or the lighting of candles. It is not enough for a person to feel her grief. Healthy grief must involve mourning.

Myth #2: The grief process is orderly and predictable.

Dr. Elizabeth Kubler-Ross, in her groundbreaking book, *On Death and Dying* (1973), laid out for us the stages of grief—denial, anger, bargaining, depression, and acceptance. The myth is that every grief experience will follow this orderly progression, from stage 1 to stage 5. That is not what Dr. Kubler-Ross was trying to express! Although these stages are real, everyone grieves in his own unique way, and it is most frequently an uneven process. There are many factors that affect our mourning—our relationship with the person who died, the circumstances surrounding the death, age, culture, faith, etc.

Myth #3: The best thing one can do is to keep busy and avoid the pain of grief.

We are typically taught that pain is an indication that something is wrong and that we should find ways to alleviate the pain. In grief, the opposite is true. The best thing one can do in grief is to open themselves to the presence of their pain. Crazy as it sounds, a grieving person's pain is the key that opens their heart and moves them forward on their way to healing. Staying busy may be helpful in short-term coping by masking the pain; however, it merely postpones one's grieving.

Myth #4: The goal of mourning is to "get over it."

In working with the grieving, you will frequently hear the question, "Are they over it yet?" or "When will I ever get over this?" Or, even worse, "They should be over it by now and get on with life!" Even though other people want the mourner to get over his grief because it will make them feel better, it is not going to happen. Rather, the one grieving will learn to move forward and enjoy life again, in spite of the pain of loss that will always be there.

Myth #5: Tears and other displays of emotion are a sign of weakness.

Crying is a wonderful way to mourn a loss—to release the pain inside. This is true for both women and men, and in no way shows a sign of weakness. Quite the contrary, it takes a strong man to face his emotions and to let them out through his tears. Look at the way that God regards your emotions. Psalm 56:8 (CEV) says, "You have stored my tears in your bottle and counted each of them." The Lord God, ruler of the universe, tenderly collects the tears you shed. He saves them all and records each of them in His eternal record. That is how important your emotions are!

Myth #6: Grief is only an emotional reaction.

Grief affects a person in far more ways than emotionally. A few examples of the different responses to the experience of grief are hyperactivity or hypoactivity, insomnia or sleeping all the time, and uncontrolled appetite or having no appetite at all. A comment I regularly hear people make is that they never knew how painful grief can be.

Myth #7: Nobody can help you with your grief.

The truth is, those in the midst of grief need other people—supportive people who understand the process of grief—to talk to, to listen to their story. This is why end-of-life coaches are so much in need! Many find this help in grief support groups as well. (See chapter 10 for further words on this form of group coaching.)

Myth #8: Time heals all wounds.

Although this old cliché is stated often, the truth of the matter is that time alone has nothing to do with healing. To heal one must mourn and walk through the grief journey. It is true that this journey takes time, but unless one does the work of mourning, the time itself will accomplish nothing but to prolong the grief.

Myth #9: Moving on with your life means you're forgetting the one you lost.

We never get over our grief, but we can reconcile it and move forward with a meaningful life. This can be very honoring to our loved one. We will continue to remember them as we discover our "new normal."

Myth #10: Grief finally ends.

This myth says that when we do all the right things, and grief and mourning are finally reconciled, they will never come up again. This is not true. Even many years following a death, deep bursts of grief pain are common.

I recently visited one of my hospice patients, who was typically a very cheery and happy person. This particular day when I walked in, she was crying hysterically. I asked what had happened. She said, "I miss my mom." She had just attended a special service at the facility where she lives. It brought back memories of her mom. I asked when her mom died, and she told me her mom died in a plague when my patient was six years old. My patient is currently 97 years old. Her mother died 91 years ago, and on this day she was crying hysterically because she missed her. This is perfectly normal, healthy grief. My patient was doing well!

In order to coach a person who is at end of life—whether they are dying or are grieving the death of a loved one, it is imperative that the end-of-life coach understands what it means to have their clients doing well.

Chapter Six

Coached, Not Counseled

The traditional model of caring for a person at end of life has always been to counsel them. A person who struggled with his terminal illness was visited by a therapist. An individual struggling in her grief was sent to see a grief counselor. Counselors are not bad in dealing with end-of-life issues. When a dying person is struggling with a major issue, such as an unresolved matter from the past, a therapist is exactly who I would like her to see. When an individual is dealing with complicated grief issues, there is no one better to help him than a grief counselor. But for an individual dealing with a typical end-of-life issue, which we will inevit-ably all experience, there is no one better to turn to than an end-of-life coach.

Our basic coaching courses taught us the difference between coaching and counseling. (For review, see Val's section entitled "Coaching Versus Therapy" on pages 8-10 of *The Next Great Awakening* (2010).) At end of life, the coach and the counselor approach situations with different mindsets. (See table on next page.)

In the counseling mindset, the purpose and objective of meeting with someone is to help them feel better. Typically, that is why the counselor is called in. The woman who is dying might be feeling depressed about what is happening to her and what she knows will happen. The counselor steps in to help her get over her depression.

When my father was first put onto hospice, he already had one leg amputated and was planning to have his second leg amputated. Now he was told that his heart was giving out and that hospice would be the best option. After talking it all through and helping my father sign all the necessary paperwork, I heard his one nurse say to another nurse, "Mr. Eisenhauer seems depressed. Call the therapist to come give him a psych consult. We need to see if we can make him feel better."

I went out to talk to her and said, "Are you kidding me? Dad is planning to have his second leg amputated to alleviate some of his pain. He was just told that he is dying, and signed papers for hospice. He has every right to feel depressed. Please allow him to do so." Dad was beginning to grieve what he had already lost, and what he was going to lose. He needed some time to mourn. Understand, there is nothing wrong with sending a patient for a psych consult. Nor is it wrong for a patient to be given medication to help with his depression. But the last thing my father needed at that moment was to have someone try to make him feel better. He needed to grieve. He needed to face the pain he was feeling, and to let it out.

End of Life Counselor's Mindset vs. Coach's Mindset	
Counselor's Mindset	**Coach's Mindset**
Make you feel better	Encourage you to embrace the pain and feelings
Help you get over your grief	Walk the journey with you through your grief
Lead you to the place where they think you should be	Walk alongside you, wherever you happen to be
Analyze with his or her head how you are doing	Listen with his/her heart as to what you are experiencing
Give you the answers to all your physical, emotional, and spiritual questions	Affirm you and empower you, as you work through all your physical, emotional and spiritual questions
Goal is to get you back to "normal"	Celebrate with you the discovery of your "new normal"

The person who has had a loved one die seeks out a grief counselor because they don't feel like they are handling their grief well, and they want to feel better. "Help me get over this," they will often say. And the counselor's goal is to do just that—to make them feel better, and to help them get over their grief.

In the process of helping, the counselor will lead their client to the place where he, the counselor, thinks the client should be at that moment. The counselor takes the lead. The counselor sets the direction. The counselor has the client's destination (outcome) in mind.

The whole time they are talking, the counselor analyzes with his or her head how the client is doing, making adjustments as to the right therapy needed.

As questions are raised, the counselor does everything possible to answer those questions, whether they be physical, emotional, or spiritual. The counselor is the "expert," you see, the one who has the insights needed and the answers that are sought. He or she is the one who is above their client, the one who is being called in to give direction.

And the ultimate goal of the counselor is to get the person struggling with an end-of-life issue back to normal. It is to get the dying person to approach death like their old selves. Or, it is to help the grieving individual get back to normal, the way they were before their loved one died.

Please understand that in this description, I am not trying to put down counselors. As stated earlier, there is a time and place for counselors at end of life. I consider myself one of them. There have been occasions when, because of some unresolved issues from the past, or some complicated grief issues in the present, instead of coaching an individual at end of life, I have been their therapist. But understand that this is not the norm. The mindset of the counselor is totally different than that of a coach and, in my opinion, providing therapy is not usually the preferred method for helping the person dealing with an end-of-life issue.

Contrast the counseling mindset to the mindset of the coach. In the coach's thinking, the purpose and objective of meeting with someone at end of life is not to make them feel better, but to encourage them to embrace their pain and feelings. In comparison, the end-of-life coach joins to walk the journey through their client's grief. That word "through" is important. I sometimes compare the journey of grief to a tunnel. Tunnels are not fun places. They are dark and scary. But the only way to get to the other side is to walk through.

I also love that phrase, "walk the journey." End of life is a journey. It is a journey toward death (and life beyond death), or it is a journey through grief. The mindset of the coach is always to walk that journey, wherever it leads, alongside of their client.

Where the counselor will lead their client to the counselor's goal, the coaching mindset allows the client to take the lead. The coachee sets the direction. The coachee has their own destination (outcome) in mind, as to where they want to be. The coach walks alongside of them, supporting them on the journey.

The whole time they are talking, while the counselor analyzes with his or her head how the client is doing, the coach listens with his or her heart as to what the client is experiencing.

As questions are raised, the coach does everything possible to affirm and empower their clients to work through all the physical, emotional, and spiritual questions that are normal to be asking at this time. The coach is the "student," while the client is the expert. It is believed that they have within themselves everything that they need to walk through their journey. And the coach is right there beside them as they do so.

The ultimate goal of the coach is to celebrate with their clients as they discover their "new normal." In dealing with end-of-life issues, one never goes back to where they were. They never get back to "normal." End-of-life issues change a person forever. It can be a positive change. End-of-life issues can bring much growth and transformation, which needs to be affirmed and celebrated.

End-of-life counselors can be helpful and are needed. But what most people need more is an end-of-life coach to walk the journey with them.

As Val wrote, coaching is a partnership. This partnership will be focused 100% on the person being coached, and will build a safe and trusting relationship where anything and everything can be shared (Hastings 2010, 6). This is the end-of-life coach's mindset!

Chapter Seven

Coaching the Dying

So, practically, what does the end-of-life coach need to do in order to honor this partnership and to walk the journey toward death (and eternal life), and through grief, with our coachees?

The place to start is by remembering "The Eight Building Blocks." An end-of-life coaching session (a visit or phone conversation) is still a coaching session and, so, the eight building blocks must provide the framework for our coaching.

Beyond that, in the pages that follow, you will discover "Eight Supporting Building Blocks" specifically related to coaching the dying, and "Eight Supporting Building Blocks" specifically related to coaching the grieving.

The Eight Building Blocks

Let me begin with a brief review of the Eight Building Blocks. (For a more complete review, see Appendix II, "The Eight Building Blocks of Coaching.")

1) Deep Listening

All coaching begins with listening! This is true for end-of-life care, as well as any coaching session. If we don't first listen deeply, we will never be able to partner with them and to walk the journey beside them. It is by listening that we allow them to take the lead.

2) Powerful Questioning

As with all coaching, powerful questions are one of the end-of-life coach's greatest tools. It is through powerful questions that the coachee is encouraged to share deeply from the heart, to explore new possibilities, and to consider what is right for them.

3) Artful Language

In end-of-life care, more than ever, our words matter. Those dealing with end-of-life issues will hear a lot of negative words directed their way, criticizing where they are on their journey, and pushing them to be someplace that they are not. The end-of-life coach must use words that will express acceptance and understanding, and bring hope and support.

4) Action and Accountability

The three components of brainstorming, designing the action, and follow through are all important in coaching at end of life. This building block helps the coachee discover different perspectives and possibilities. It enables them to rise above their current situation to see the bigger picture.

5) The Coaching Relationship

Relating, relating, relating! Providing a safe and supportive environment is always important in coaching, but never more so than in coaching at end of life. This is so true that we will explore it deeper in the first supporting building block for both the dying and the grieving.

6) The Coaching Agreement

Since the coachee is the one who takes the lead in walking the journey, the coaching agreement is the means by which they express their desires and goals. Be reminded of the ongoing nature of the coaching agreement, including the initial agreement, the ongoing agreement and the evaluation process.

7) Creating New Awareness

Because end-of-life issues are rarely discussed in our culture and myths abound, we must create new awareness for our coachees. This will be developed further in our supporting building blocks.

8) Direct Communication

Using clear, concise, laser-like words, along with offering one question or statement at a time, helps greatly in communicating with our coachees. Because of the intensity of the issues involved in end-of-life care, appropriate silence and pauses are a must. Tapping into a person's greatness can also be very affirming, because during this time they are typically not feeling very much greatness.

The Eight Supporting Building Blocks for Coaching the Dying

Keeping in mind the eight building blocks, I now want to add eight supporting building blocks for coaching the dying.

1) Provide A Safe Place

Even though providing a safe and supportive environment is already a part of the coaching relationship basic building block, it is listed here for added emphasis. Every coaching session needs to take place in a setting where the coachee feels safe and comfortable to share openly. When you are coaching someone who is dying, this is magnified many times over. And it takes more than just saying, "This is a safe place where you can share anything you want." It will take action. You will need to prove to your dying coachee that this really is a safe place to share. And they will probably test you on it.

The person who is dying is most likely experiencing a wide variety of feelings/emotions/issues, such as sadness and despair, grief, anger, anxiety, the effects and symptoms of physical pain, fear, guilt, and spiritual questions, to name just a few. They might be clinging to life, or they might be longing to die right now. They might be prepared to die, or they might feel totally lost and overwhelmed.

Anything Is Acceptable

Whatever it is that the dying person is feeling or experiencing, they need to know it is okay for them to talk about it without you reacting in negative ways. As I said, they will probably test you on it. The first time you react in a negative way, you are telling them this is NOT a safe place for them to talk, and that will hinder your ministry to them. Some of the negative reactions include:

- **Shutting them down.** When something negative is shared, such as "I wish I would die right now," many will respond, "Oh don't talk that way!" Right then, they need to talk that way. If you shut them down, they realize you are not a safe place to be real.

- **Defending God.** In expressing their feelings, it is common for a dying person to question God, or even curse God. If you listen to what they share, affirm what they are saying, and validate the feelings behind their words, you will encourage them to keep on talking. If you start to defend God, you will declare that place unsafe!

- **An unwillingness to face realities.** Some don't like to hear or accept that another could be dying. One might respond, "God will perform a miracle," or "You have to think positively," or "Don't give up yet; stop talking that way!" Just because you, as a coach, are dealing with the realities, does not mean that you are keeping God from performing a miracle. Most dying people want to face the realities and want to talk them through. The only way that will be possible, however, is if you provide a safe place for them to do that.

They Don't Need To Be Fixed

Not only does your dying coachee need a safe place where they can share openly, they need to know that you are not going to try to "fix them" when they do so. The reality is, when the dying openly share their feelings, emotions and experiences, they don't need to be fixed. They need to be listened to, and affirmed and accepted. When they have the opportunity to get these things out, they will usually have the resources within themselves to sort through what they are saying and to "fix" themselves. But it starts with them simply getting it out.

Entertain Their Favorite Question

As coaches, we love questions! Well your dying coachees will probably have a lot of questions, themselves. And most of the time, their favorite question is a little three letter word—Why? You will know that you are doing well as a coach when you don't feel the need to answer their question, but rather, to encourage them to keep asking it. Most of the time, they are not really wanting an answer or explanation as to why this or that is happening. Most of the time, the "why" questions are a way of expressing their feelings or pain. If you try to answer their questions, or even worse, tell them they should not question "why," you will miss out on a wonderful opportunity to address the deeper feelings that are present.

2) Be Present With Them

Earlier in the book, I shared that people often stay far away from a dying person because of their fear. They are afraid they will not know what to say or to do, so they don't even try.

The reality is that the most important ministry you can perform for the dying, and for their family or caregivers, is the ministry of presence. Your being present with them will mean more than anything you could ever say or do! This becomes especially true, because so many stay away!

In his book *Dying Well* (1998), palliative care physician Ira Byock, MD, wrote, "While I may bring clinical skills and years of experience to the task, ultimately I am simply present, offering to help and wanting to learn." Coaching the dying is far more about a way of being in the presence of a dying coachee than it is following specific techniques to minister to them.

Work Through Your Own Issues of Death and Dying

Before you can be truly present with a dying coachee, you must work through your own issues related to death and dying. The process for doing that will be described in more detail in chapter 11 of this book. For now, it is enough to say that, until you work through your own personal issues, you will never be able to be truly present with the dying. Your focus will always be on yourself, your feelings, your reactions, your fears, your death experiences. How freeing, both for you and for your coachee and family, when you can be truly present with them. That's when real ministry takes place!

Be Still

Coaching is all about moving forward! This is still true when it comes to coaching the dying. However, before an end-of-life coach can move forward with his/her dying coachee, there often needs to be a time of being still. Sometimes the whole time together, session after session, can be times of being still. This can be very powerful, and is not a coaching failure. Often it is exactly what the dying coachee needs.

Psalm 46:10 says, "Be still (cease striving!) and know that I am God." There are times when we need to cease striving, to stop, and to be still in the presence of God. Your dying coachee will need those times, too—to be still before God, and to be still in the midst of the chaos around them. The activity around a dying person is often so frantic, stillness will be a treasured gift you bring. Where your natural tendency will be to think, "I can't just sit here; I must do something!" Instead, remind yourself, "I can't just do something; I must sit here!" That is stillness.

Stillness allows time for personal reflection about all that is going on. Stillness allows the dying to initiate their own coaching agreement—what they need, when they are ready to go there, how fast they will travel, and what their destination is. This is their journey. We are there to walk beside them, not to lead them. Stillness allows the dying to be in control. As a person declines physically, they often find themselves losing control in so many areas, and there is nothing they can do about it. Giving them something to control, such as your visit with them, is yet another gift you bring.

One final reason for stillness is a very practical one. As their body declines and gets weaker, it is common for dying coachees to become slow in their verbal responses. It takes time for them to build up enough energy or to breathe well enough to get their words out. The stillness gives them the opportunity to respond without pressure or the feeling of being rushed.

Allow for Silence

Following closely behind the encouragement to be still is the reminder to allow for silence. This is part of the direct communication basic building block, which we learn in introductory coaching. With your dying coachees, however, the silence is often more pronounced and can last a lot longer. It will be a great day when you become comfortable with this silence and see it as a tool for ministry, rather than as an awkward moment.

The Presence of God

One final point is the reminder that when you are truly present with your dying coachee, you become a living example of God's ever abiding presence. I can't think of anything that they need more, or that could be more important in ministering to them.

All through Scripture, God's comfort and strength in the midst of difficult times came by means of His presence with His people. When God spoke to Moses through the burning bush, he said to him, "I am sending you to Pharaoh to bring my people the Israelites out of Egypt." But Moses said to God, "Who am I that I should go to Pharaoh and bring the Israelites out of Egypt?" And God said, "I will be with you" (Ex 3:10-12). When the Lord commanded Joshua to lead the Israelites into the Promised Land, He said to him, "Be strong and courageous. Do not be afraid; do not be discouraged, for the LORD your God will be with you wherever you go" (Joshua 1:9). In the great commission, Jesus said to His disciples,

> All authority in heaven and on earth has been given to me. Therefore go and make disciples of all nations, baptizing them in the name of the Father and of the Son and of the Holy Spirit, and teaching them to obey everything I have commanded you. And surely I am with you always, to the very end of the age (Matt. 28:18-20).

What an amazing privilege it is to remind a dying person of God's presence with them.

3) Invite Them to Tell Their Story

When they have tested and proven that they are in a safe place, and sense that you truly are present with them, the dying coachee might be willing to go deeper with you. To aid them in this process, it is helpful to invite them to tell you their story.

Most people facing death love to tell their story. They find telling their story to be healing and refreshing. Their story might be a recounting of what they are experiencing right now. Perhaps it will be the story of their disease process. Their story might be a description of what a loved one is experiencing, or how they are reacting to their changing condition. It could be a recounting of the past, or a sharing of their dreams or fears of the future. Whatever is pressing upon their hearts and minds at that time is their story. And when the dying begin to open up and share their story with you, those moments become sacred. The dying are sharing the deepest parts of themselves with you. They are sharing their life. The end-of-life coach would do well to listen attentively!

Life Review

Part of the reason why the dying find it so important to tell their story is because it becomes the means by which they review their lives for meaning. We call this "life review." As the dying reflect on past and present times, they are evaluating what their life has been like, whether or not it was meaningful, and determining in what ways they made a contribution and a difference. They are also reminding themselves of who they really are. "I am John Smith, who has lived an active life and has made a difference in this world. This cancer does not define the person I am, my life does!" The end-of-life coach, through active listening, inviting curiosity, and strong questioning, can aid them in this sacred process. It can be a powerful and meaningful time!

Some of the powerful questions that can help in the invitation for the dying to share their stories might be as follows:

- So, what have you been thinking about lately as you sit here in your chair?
- When it gets quiet, what does your mind turn to?
- What is this like for you?

Some dying coachees will want to go a step further than just talking through their life story. Some find it helpful to journal. Some will journal in their own free time, often in the middle of the night when they awaken, and then read what they wrote to their coach at a later time. Others will find it helpful to make up a photo album, gathering pictures of their life story.

It is their story. Whatever will help the dying tell their story is what they should do. It is helpful, however, for the coach to have some of these possibilities in mind to share with their coachees as options to choose from.

Their Faith Story

Another aspect of "their story," which the dying typically want to share, is their faith story. My experience has shown that 99.9% of the dying people I have coached long to share their faith story—even those who have never been part of a church and have never in their life been interested in spiritual things. When one knows that they are dying, spiritual things all of a sudden become very important. Often, they are longing to talk about their faith story and are not sure how to bring it up.

Some of the powerful questions that can help in the invitation for the dying to share their faith stories might be as follows:

- When things get really bad, where do you find your help and strength?

- What brings you meaning during this time?

- What is going to happen to you after you die?

We will talk more about addressing their faith stories in supporting building block #8, but for now, the encouragement is simply to invite them to share.

Their Bucket List

The term "Bucket List" was made popular in the 2007 film by that title, starring Jack Nicholson and Morgan Freeman. These two terminally ill men, who share a hospital room, define a list of things to do before they "kick the bucket." It can be very helpful to ask your dying coachee what is on their bucket list. For one, it gets them to share more of what is important to them. But secondly, it gives them some practical things for them to work toward accomplishing. Be advised that, as their body declines, their list might have to be adjusted to fit reasonable expectations. This can be a discouraging time for the dying. They realize they can no longer accomplish some of the things on their list. The end-of-life coach becomes a great encouragement here, after listening to their pain, to help them to rewrite their list as to what they still can do. Here the basic building block "Action and Accountability" comes in, taking it to the next level of helping them to decide how and when they are going to do them, and who will help and support them in carrying them out.

Funeral Preparation

Another aspect of "their story" is thoughts concerning their funeral. Often this topic will not be brought up by the coachee themselves, but when the coach initiates the conversation, the coachee is eager to discuss it. Once again, this is your coachee's story, so if they do not wish to discuss their funeral, it is very much okay. In most cases, however, the dying want to talk about it. It is the rest of the family and friends who are not willing to "go there" with them.

Allowing the dying to talk about this aspect of their story is helpful for the dying and for their families, who will need to make funeral arrangements. If the family is not present for this conversation, ask permission to take notes and to share the information with them.

For some of our dying coachees, this is what they need more than anything else. They need a safe place, with their coach being truly present, where they can share their story—even the parts that no one else wants to hear. Sometimes their stories will go on and on and on. Sometimes their stories will be repeats of what they shared during their last session. That is OK. The purpose isn't so much to give you new information, as it is for them to share their story—and often that involves many takes!

Many people will not take the time to listen to the dying. Many will be afraid of what they might hear. Many will be too emotional and will not be able to listen without breaking down.

The end-of-life coach makes it clear that they love to hear their dying coachees' stories, and they invite them to share.

4) Discover Their Most Precious Possession

The dying realize that the time they have left on this earth is short. As a result, they typically will let go of those things that are not as important to them. They want to use the limited time and energy they have to focus on the things that are most important. As the end-of-life coach listens to their dying coachee's story, it will become evident what their most precious possession is. Once again, my experience has shown that 99.9% of the dying people I have coached have clearly identified people—the people in their lives (family, friends)—as their most precious possession.

The end-of-life coach will do well to listen for this and, if it is not heard, to inquire about it. Who are the people in their lives? What are their relationships like? What does your dying coachee love/desire/need concerning these individuals?

Typically, this is a topic the dying love to talk about more than anything else. They love to brag about their family members. They want to share the pain of the ones who are hurting.

They want to grieve relationships that are lost. When their most precious possession comes up in their sharing, the end-of-life coach will do well to say to them, "Tell me more …"

Time with Those They Love

Because "the people in their lives" usually are their most precious possession, spending time with these individuals is usually what they desire more than anything else. Listen for what they share about this. Are they content with the time they are spending? Do they desire more? Who do they want time with? Are there certain things they want to say to them? Do with them? How will they go about contacting them, and when will they do it?

Reconciliation

Earlier in the book, I stated that a "good death" involves two things – a death that goes well, and a person who is well when they die. A dying person is not well when they have people in their lives with whom they need reconciliation. This is especially true when those people are family members. A lot of energy is spent on wanting to reconcile those relationships before your coachee dies. The end-of-life coach can play a big role in encouraging this process, and allowing the dying to talk through how this will be accomplished. Most times reconciliation is possible, although sometimes, when the other person involved is not willing, it is not possible. Both scenarios will need to be processed by the dying one.

Making Sure They Are Cared For

Another typical concern of the dying is making sure their most precious possession will be cared for after they die. A lot of energy goes into this concern, and the dying are not "well" until they feel comfortable in this area. Sometimes the dying will "hold on" and not allow themselves to die, because this concern is still so heavy on their heart.

Although this concern is so real, some dying coachees have trouble expressing it, especially to their loved one. The end-of-life coach can be a great help in this area, helping your coachee to talk it through. The coach can even help bring the two parties together and coach them through this process.

The concerns for care cover many areas:

• **Physical and Emotional.** When my father was dying, he asked me to care for my mom and wanted to hear me say that I would do so. He wanted to know someone else would be watching over her.

- **Financial.** The dying want to know their loved ones will be able to survive financially and often have ideas of things they can do to ensure this will happen.

- **Practical.** There are many practical concerns the dying want settled. If they are the ones who handled the finances, or prepared the taxes, or did the laundry, or cooked all the meals, they want their loved ones to know how to take over these things. They want to inform their loved ones where the important documents are kept, or which banks hold their accounts, or what kind of oil goes into the car.

- **Legal.** If the dying never wrote up a will, the end-of-life coach can help them know how to facilitate this process. If a car is in your dying coachee's name, it is far easier to transfer the car into their loved one's name while they are still living.

- **Medical.** A living will declares a person's wishes for when they become seriously ill. A helpful resource to set up a living will is "Five Wishes." "Five Wishes" allows the dying to declare their wish for:

  1. The person they want to make care decisions for them when they can't;

  2. The kind of medical treatment they want or don't want;

  3. How comfortable they want to be;

  4. How they want people to treat them; and

  5. What they want their loved ones to know.

  This resource can be obtained at www.agingwithdignity.org.

- **Material.** Sometimes there are specific objects that are not specified in the will that they want specific family members to have. My father loved his lawn tractor. Some of my best memories of him in his later years are on that tractor. Before he died, he told me it was now time for me to take his tractor.

  One coachee, after she and I talked through this topic, decided to call all of her family members to her home. She told them that she wanted to pass on her material things to all of them, but she didn't want them to fight over her things. So she took out her sticky pad, and one by one she gave a sticky to a family member, and invited them to "tag" an item as theirs to take after she was gone. She continued this until everything was tagged. It gave this dying coachee great peace to know this was handled peacefully while she was still alive.

- **Spiritual.** See Ethical Wills below.

Ethical Wills

A regular, legal will declares how an individual's material and financial goods will be distributed after they die. Wills are important, and I believe everyone should have a will. The problem, however, is that a will doesn't pass on that which was most important to the deceased. At the end of their lives, most individuals come to the conclusion that their material possessions are not what is most important. Their values (spiritual, relational, and moral) are more important than the dollars in their bank. They want to pass on their spiritual beliefs and desires, and hopes and dreams for those who are left behind.

Your end-of-life coachee might want to talk about these things, and you can invite them to do so. Taking this a step further, you can help them pass these things on to those who remain, through the means of an "ethical will." An ethical will is not a legal document. Rather, it is the act of leaving behind those things that are of most importance.

An ethical will could be established in the following ways:

- Invite your dying coachee to write down those things they want their most precious possessions to remember about them. This could be done in the form of a letter written to each individual.

- Tape record the dying sharing, in their own words, the values and beliefs they are leaving behind, and what it is that they desire for their loved ones.

- Produce a DVD of your client sharing what was most important to them. I did this for a number of my end-of-life coaching clients. I videotaped them sharing their hearts with their loved ones. Some of my dying coachees spoke in generalities, while others spoke specifically to each member of the family, sharing personal and specific hopes and dreams and desires for them. I then turned this video into a DVD. Some of my clients directed me to give the DVD immediately to their family members. Other clients asked me to hold onto the DVD until after they had died and to then give it to their family members. In the case of the latter, my dying clients began their DVD by saying, "The fact that you are watching this means that I have died..."

Families have found a DVD like this to be very meaningful. The coachee feels great satisfaction because he shares deeply from his heart.

Final Contacts

Before a person dies, it is common for them to want to make final contact with each of their most precious possessions. I have seen numerous dying coachees hold onto life until a loved one has arrived from out of town. Sometimes the dying were no longer strong enough to speak. They knew a loved one was coming, and they waited to die until the out-of-towner arrived. When a physical visit isn't possible, a final phone call will often suffice. Even when the dying can no longer speak, we can hold the phone to their ear. This can be enough to give them peace and to allow them to die well. It is beneficial for the end-of-life coach to be aware of this possibility.

5) Help Them Share "The Five Things"

John Mayer wrote a wonderful song entitled, "Say What You Need to Say." This concept is the focus of the fifth supporting building block for coaching the dying.

One of the great privileges we have as human beings is the ability to communicate verbally. The end-of-life coach will do well to encourage his dying coachee and family to take advantage of this privilege. (Where the previous supporting building blocks focused specifically on the dying coachee, this one focuses on the coachee in relation to his family.) This is the time to "say what they need to say." There is no topic off limits. It is the perfect time for the dying and their loved ones to share what is in their hearts.

The coach can remind everyone present that this time together prior to the death is an opportunity that some families never get. Many wish they had the opportunity to share their hearts with their loved ones before they die, but never get that opportunity.

People will often ask, "What are good things to talk about at this time?" I remind them that they can share anything and everything—thoughts, memories, fears, hopes, dreams…. There are five things, however, that I have found to be most helpful at this time.

"The Five Things" are adapted from a book by Ira Byock, MD, *The Four Things That Matter Most* (2004). They are as follows:

1. Please Forgive Me
2. I Forgive You
3. Thank You
4. I Love You
5. Good-Bye

When I coach a dying person or family, I will ask permission to share these five things. "I will tell you what the five things are, then you can do with them as you desire." I will explain:

1. **Please forgive me.** Because you are a human being, you make mistakes just like we all do. It makes an incredible difference to know that you have asked for forgiveness for those things.

2. **I forgive you.** No matter how wonderful your loved one is, he is a human being, too, and therefore also isn't perfect. You give him a wonderful gift by declaring that you hold nothing against him and that he is forgiven.

3. **Thank you.** Thank you for the times when … Thank you for being the person who …

4. **I love you.** Some people find it easy to say those words, while others find it difficult. If you love this person, it is important to tell them.

5. **Good-bye.** This is the one a lot of families struggle with. They will often tear up when I say the word. I ask them, "Do you know where the word good-bye originally comes from? It comes from the phrase, 'God be with ye,' which eventually got shortened to good-bye. When you are saying good-bye, what you are really saying is, 'God be with you' and 'I entrust you to God's care until I see you again.'" I invite them to say this to their loved one every time they part. "I entrust you to God's care, until I come back in the morning." "Good-bye. God be with you until I return from the kitchen." One of the greatest regrets many people have is not being able to say good-bye to their loved one before they die. If they establish the habit, when the time of the final good-bye arrives ("until I see you in heaven"), the survivor knows the farewells were shared.

I have shared "The Five Things" with my coachees and their families for many years now. Positive feedback abounds. Families tell me over and over what a help it was to talk about these five things with their loved ones. Those in the midst of grief regularly share that they can move forward because they "said what they need to say."

When my father went onto hospice, I had already been in the habit of sharing "The Five Things" with people. I had never, however, shared what they were with my father. My father was a Pennsylvania Dutchman. Common to that heritage, he did not openly share his feelings. Yet, when he knew he was dying, my father shared with me every one of those five things without any prompting.

Your dying coachees want to talk about these things. Their families need to talk about them. You, as an end-of-life coach, are in a wonderful position to be able to invite them to do so. Verbal communication truly is a wonderful privilege and a gift.

All too often, unfortunately, we take this gift for granted. There is no time when this becomes more apparent than when a family is with a loved one who can no longer speak.

When the body is dying, it is common for the dying person to get so weak that they can no longer speak. The body has only so much strength left and all of the energy goes to keeping the major organs of the body functioning. As a result, it is difficult for the individual to move, and it is often impossible for them to speak. This can be difficult for families who have not yet shared "The Five Things". They still want to communicate with their loved one. There is more they desire to say. There is more they want to hear their loved one say to them.

The good news is that it takes almost no energy for a person to listen – to use their ears. What that means is that even when the person is too weak to move or speak, they can still hear. I believe they can hear right up until the moment they cease to breathe. When my father was actively dying and could no longer speak, my mother and I gathered around him. We talked to Dad and shared our hearts with him. We again shared "The Five Things". When we finished speaking, we saw a tear come out of Dad's eye. I believe that was the only way Dad was able to respond to us at that time, but through that tear, he showed that he heard everything we said.

Even when your dying coachee can no longer speak, it is not too late to share "The Five Things". Informing families of this can bring great comfort.

6) Assure Them with What Is Normal

I have now had the privilege of coaching literally thousands of people who were dying. They all had one thing in common. None of them had died before. 100% of those with whom I have walked the journey toward death were in uncharted territory.

Chances are those dying individuals to whom you will minister will not be experts at dying either. The only way you can be an expert at dying is by dying. There aren't too many of those individuals around.

When we do anything for the first time, the normal reaction is to experience fear and anxiety concerning how the uncharted territory will look. We have a lot of questions about the unknown, wondering what the process of death will be like. Even when we are going through the new experience, we question whether we are doing it right. We wonder if anyone else has ever experienced what we are experiencing. We are unsure as to how family/caregivers should respond. We ponder whether or not our journey is "normal."

The end-of-life coach, who is educated in this matter, can be a source of great comfort and support to his coachees. Sometimes all they need to hear is that what they are experiencing is normal. Their families will be struggling with the same questions and will also be comforted by your words of wisdom.

Clearly I am not an expert in dying either. However, I have spent an extensive amount of time with the experts. I would like to share with you some of the "normal" experiences that one goes through as he or she approaches the end of his or her life.

Below are the signs which precede death in most people as their body systems slow down and finally cease functioning. For some people, these signs appear a few hours before death. For others, these signs may begin to appear several days or even weeks before death. There is no particular order in which these events occur, and some people will not experience all of them.

When a person enters the final stage of the dying process, two different interrelated and interdependent dynamics are at work. On the physical plane, the body begins the final process of shutting down, which will end when all the physical systems cease to function. Usually, this is an orderly and undramatic series of physical changes which are not medical emergencies. They are a normal, natural way in which the body prepares itself to stop working. The best way one can assist with these changes is by helping the loved one feel comfortable and secure.

The other dynamic of the dying process is the emotional-spiritual-mental plane. The "spirit" of the dying person begins the final process of release from the body. This release also tends to follow its own priorities. This may include unfinished business and reception of permission to "let go" from family and other loved ones. These "events" are the natural way in which the spirit prepares to move from this existence into the next dimension of life. The most appropriate kinds of responses to the emotional-spiritual-mental changes are those which support and encourage this release and transition.

When a person's body is ready to stop functioning, but the person is still unresolved or unreconciled over some important issue or with some significant relationship, he or she may tend to linger in order to finish whatever needs finishing. On the other hand, when a person is emotionally-spiritually-mentally resolved and ready for this release, but his or her body has not completed its final physical shutdown, the person will continue to live until that shutdown process ceases.

The experience we call death occurs when the body completes its natural process of shutting down, and the "spirit" completes its natural process of reconciling and finishing. These two processes need to happen in a way appropriate and unique to the values, beliefs and life-style of the dying person. Intermingled in all of this, I believe, is the sovereignty of God at work.

Your support and understanding as an end-of-life coach will help your coachee (and family) accomplish the transition. This is the greatest gift you have to offer as death approaches.

The physical and emotional-spiritual-mental signs and symptoms of impending death which follow are offered to help you understand the natural kinds of things which may happen and how you and/or the family can respond appropriately. Again, not all these signs and symptoms will occur with every person, nor will they occur in any particular sequence. Each person is unique and needs to do things in his/her own way.

The following signs and symptoms describe how the body prepares itself for the final stage of life:

1. **Fluid and Food Decrease.** The person may have a decrease in appetite and thirst, wanting little or no food or fluid. The body will naturally begin to conserve energy, which is expended on nourishment. Do not try to force food or drink into the person, or try to use guilt to manipulate them into eating or drinking something. Since normal hydration is often not feasible, it is more peaceful for the body to decline in a state of dehydration than fluid overload. Small chips of ice or frozen juices/popsicles may be refreshing in the mouth. Be careful of decreases in swallowing ability. Do not force fluids if the person coughs soon after intake. The reflexes needed to swallow may become sluggish. This is how the person's body lets him or her know when it no longer wants or can tolerate food or liquids. The loss of this desire for food and drink may be a signal that the person is getting ready to die. Swabs may be used to keep the mouth/lips moist and comfortable.

2. **Decreased Socialization.** The person may want to be alone, with just one person, or with very few people. Naturally, you don't feel like socializing when you're weak and tired. Our words can sometimes arouse a person to be present with us, so be careful to allow quality rest time as much as possible. Reassure the person it is okay to sleep. If you are not part of this inner circle at the end, it does not mean you are not loved or are unimportant. It means you have already fulfilled your task with your loved one, and it is time for you to say good-bye. If you are part of

the final inner circle of support, the person needs your affirmation, support, and permission to die. Also take note that it is common for a person to choose to die alone. I have watched family after family sit by their dying loved one around the clock. It is not until the family member gets up to go to the bathroom or to walk outside to get the mail that the dying breathes his last breath. Even though it is not typically painful to watch someone die, I believe this is one final gift the dying person is giving to his family.

3. **Sleeping.** The person may spend an increasing amount of time sleeping and may appear to be uncommunicative, unresponsive and, at times, difficult to arouse. This normal change is due in part to changes in the metabolism of the body. Sit with your dying coachee, hold their hand, do not shake them or speak loudly, but rather speak softly and naturally. Plan to spend time when he or she is most alert. At this point, being with him or her is more important than doing for them. Speak directly as you normally would, even though there may be no response. Never assume that the person cannot hear; hearing is said to be the last of the senses to be lost.

4. **Restlessness.** The person may make restless and repetitive motions such as pulling at bed linen or clothing. This often happens and is due in part to the decrease in circulation to the brain and metabolic changes. Do not be alarmed, interfere, or try to restrain such motions. To have a calming effect, speak in a quiet, natural way, lightly massage the hand or forehead, read to the person, or play soothing music.

5. **Disorientation.** The person may seem confused about time, place, and identity of the people surrounding him or her, including close and familiar people. Identify yourself by name before you speak rather than asking the person to guess who you are. Speak softly, clearly, and truthfully when you need to communicate something important for the patient's comfort. For example, say, "It's time to take your medication," and explain the reason for the communication, such as, "So you won't begin to hurt."

6. **Urine Decrease.** The person's urine output normally decreases and may turn dark and resemble tea. This is a sign that the urine is becoming concentrated, a normal occurrence because of a decrease in fluid intake and slowing of blood flow through the kidneys. Also, fluid is lost during breathing and perspiration.

7. **Incontinence.** The person may lose control of urine and/or bowels as the muscles in that area begin to relax. Take care to protect the bed and encourage the family to keep your dying coachee clean and comfortable.

8. **Breathing Pattern Change.** The person's regular breathing pattern may change with the onset of a different breathing pace. One particular pattern consists of breathing irregularly with shallow respirations, or periods of no breaths for 5-30 seconds, followed by a deep breath. The person may also have periods of rapid, shallow, panting-type breathing. Sometimes there is a moaning-like sound on exhale. This is not distress, but rather the sound of air passing over relaxed vocal cords. These patterns are very common and indicate a decreased circulation in the internal organs. Elevating the head and/or turning onto the side may bring comfort. Hold their hand. Speak gently and reassuringly.

9. **Congestion.** The person may develop gurgling sounds coming from the chest like a percolator. Sometimes these sounds become very loud and they can be very distressing to hear. Watch your loved one closely and note that they are usually unaware of their bodily processes. It is probably harder for you to watch and hear than it is on the dying. Suctioning is usually ineffective and can actually increase discomfort. Raise the head of the bed so secretions pool low and therefore don't stimulate gag reflex.

10. **Color Changes.** The person's arms and legs may become cold, hot, or discolored. The underside of the body may become discolored as circulation decreases. This is a normal indication that the circulation is conserving to the core to support the most vital organs. Irregular temperatures can be the result of the brain sending unclear messages. Keep the patient warm if he or she appears cold, but do not use an electric blanket. If the person continually removes the covers, then allow them just a light covering.

11. **Vision-Like Experiences.** The person may speak or claim to have spoken to people who have already died, or to see or have seen places not presently accessible or visible to you. This does not indicate a hallucination or a drug reaction. The person is beginning to detach from this life and is being prepared for the transition so it will not be frightening. Do not contradict, explain away, belittle, or argue about what the person claims to have seen or heard. Just because you cannot see or hear it does not mean it is not real to them. Affirm his or her experience. They are normal and common.

12. **Unusual Communication.** The person may make a seemingly out of character or non sequitur statement, gesture, or request. This may indicate that he or she is ready to say good-bye and is testing you to see if you are ready to let him or her go. Accept the moment as a beautiful gift when it is offered. Kiss, hug, hold, cry, and say whatever you most need to say.

13. **Permission To Go.** The family's giving permission for their loved one to let go is not an easy task. (Doing so without making him or her feel guilty for leaving can be difficult. Sometimes the survivor tries to keep him or her with them to meet their own needs.) A dying person will commonly try to hold on, even though it brings prolonged discomfort, in order to be reassured that those left behind will be all right. The family's ability to reassure and release the dying person from this concern is the greatest gift of love they can give at this time. Helpful statements may include: "We love you enough to let you go," "We wish you peace," and "I will be all right."

14. **Saying Goodbye.** When the person is ready to die and the family is able to let go, this is the time to say good-bye in your own way. This closure allows for the final release. It may be helpful to encourage the loved one to lay in bed with the person, hold hands, and/or say everything they need to say. It may be as simple as saying, I love you. It may include recounting favorite memories, places, and activities they shared. Tears are a normal and natural part of making peace and saying good-bye. They do not need to be hidden from the dying. Tears are an expression of love.

At the Time of Death...

- Breathing ceases.
- Heartbeat ceases.
- The person cannot be aroused.
- The eyelids may be partially open with the eyes in a fixed stare.
- The mouth may fall open as the jaw relaxes.
- There is sometimes a release of bowel and bladder contents as the body relaxes.

Hopefully, this information will help you to prepare the families for this moment. If you can free them from anxiety and fear, then you can help the dying to experience the final stage of life in an atmosphere of calmness and peacefulness.

7) Be the Student, Not the Expert

Your attitude toward your coachee should be that of a student. The counselor would say, "I am the expert. I am here to help you and to fix you." The end-of-life coach says, "You are the expert. Teach me what it is like for you to go through this. Help me to understand what you are experiencing."

Approaching your dying coachee with the attitude of a student is important, first of all, for your coachee. This attitude will encourage him to share more openly and deeply with you. He will know you are interested in what he has to say. It is this student attitude which will enable him to feel safe and heard, and to take charge of his own journey.

The second reason that it is important for an end-of-life coach to approach his dying coachee with the attitude of a student is for the sake of the coach. The dying have so much to teach us!

When I began my work with the hospice, I was concerned as to what it would be like to spend so much time with people who were dying. I expected it to be draining and depressing. Quite honestly, I was dreading it. To my surprise, I loved the time spent with them. The dying know what is important. They know how to spend their time and energy. The dying teach me how to live my own life. Sometimes I think I prefer being with the dying more than the living.

You can read what I have learned from the dying in my upcoming book, *Dying To Live: Lessons Learned from the Dying*. Or, you can learn these lessons on your own, by approaching every encounter with a dying coachee as a learning opportunity. Listen to them. Learn from them. Ask them to teach you. Be the student. And they will teach you how to live.

> A good name is better than fine perfume, and the day of death better than the day of birth. It is better to go to a house of mourning than to go to a house of feasting, for death is the destiny of everyone; the living should take this to heart (Ecclesiastes 7:1-2).

8) Encourage Them to Hold Onto Hope

"It may be hard to see, but there is always hope in **HOsPicE**."

As surprising as it is for people to conceive of hope being associated with hospice, it can be just as surprising to learn that the eighth supporting building block of coaching the dying is to "encourage them to hold onto hope."

It is not the responsibility of the end-of-life coach to produce hope, or to give hope, or to push their own hope onto their coachees. Rather, the coach has the privilege of helping the dying to discover the hope they already have within and to help them keep that hope alive.

I will regularly ask the dying, "What brings you hope in the midst of all that you are experiencing?" Or, "Where do you find strength when things get really rough?"

I recently coached a 60-year-old woman who was dying of cancer. She was blind since birth. When I asked her what brought her hope, she said to me, "I am a Christian, and I know that when I die I will go to heaven. My favorite Scripture passage is where we are told that we will get to see Jesus face to face. What brings me hope is to realize after I die, I will be able to see, and that the first face I will ever look at is the face of Jesus." We talked about that every time I met with her. As she was actively dying and could no longer speak, I reminded her of her "hope." A smile came across her face, and that is how she died.

What Is Hope?

Biblical hope is an absolute; a guarantee without a doubt. It means to expect or anticipate with pleasure. (See Rom. 5:2, Col. 1:5, Titus 1:2, 2:13, 3:7.) This is the hope that my blind coachee had.

Not every dying person, however, has that strong sense of hope. As a matter of fact, many of the dying feel hopeless.

It is human nature to hang onto two basic hopes—that we can overcome illness and that we can delay death. Yet the reality for many of your coachees is that they are facing a steady medical decline and are awaiting their impending death. From their perception, there may be feelings of hopelessness.

The end-of-life coach can help them create new awareness. A definition of hope that I use says that "hope is a dynamic (alive, changing) inner power that enables transcendence (that which is beyond the ordinary range of perception) of the present situation and fosters a positive new awareness of being" (1993).

Hope is something that is constantly changing. In the beginning, your coachee might hope for a cure for their illness or for a miracle of healing to occur. As their body continues to decline, the hope might change. They might hope for the strength to accomplish some tasks, or to travel to some favorite destinations. As weakness increases, that hope might change again. Now, they might hope for their pain to decrease, or for visits from friends, or phone calls from their grandchildren. Later, they might hope to be able to stay in their own home or to be able to sleep peacefully and, eventually, to be able to die peacefully with their family present with them.

Although the hope is constantly changing, it makes all the difference in the world when the dying can hold onto hope. The end-of-life coach, through active listening and powerful questioning and affirmation, can help them to keep this hope alive.

Never Give False Hope

Hope is always based on truth. The end-of-life coach should never tell the dying or their families things that are not true as a means of encouraging hope. The dying one has a right to honestly know what is going on in his own body. Decisions regarding whether or not to seek treatment or use life support measures should be his. When the hope of the dying is different than that of the family or of the coach, it is important to remember that this is all about the coachee. We are there to walk the journey with them and to support their decisions, not impose our own ideas.

How Are They Within Themselves

"How are you?" or "How are things going?" are typical questions to ask a dying person in the opening moments spent with them. The answer to those questions, however, is usually focused on how they are doing physically. In order to encourage them to hold onto hope, the end-of-life coach needs to tap into their coachee's emotional/spiritual self. To do so, a good question to follow up with is, "And how are you doing within yourself?"

Being Inwardly Renewed

It can be helpful for the coach to remind the dying of the Apostle Paul's words to the Corinthians, where he said that even though we are outwardly wasting away, we can at the same time be inwardly getting stronger spiritually (being renewed day by day). (See 2 Corinthians 4-5.) The treasure of who we really are is housed in jars of clay which crack and break and can become of no use. The dying will understand this well. While that is happening, however, their hope can be stronger than ever. Their inner emotional strength and their relationship with God can be greater than ever before. This is something the dying will often want to reflect on and discuss.

Scripture and Prayer

For many, Scripture and prayer bring hope and inner renewal. The coach needs to be careful, however, that in their attempt to encourage hope, they don't push their own agenda onto the dying. There are times when the dying do not feel like having Scripture read. There are times when they will not be up for audible prayer. As a result, the end-of-life coach should always ask permission to read Scripture or to pray (even when the dying is one of their parishioners). They must not be offended if the dying say "no," and understand that the next time they visit, the dying might greatly appreciate those means of spiritual support.

Along those same lines, I usually discourage an end-of-life coach from carrying his Bible into a visit with the dying. The appearance of the Bible in hand conveys to the dying that you have a purpose and agenda for your visit rather than allowing the dying to set the agenda. Keeping a Bible in your pocket or purse, or on your cell phone, all of which can be easily accessed when desired, creates a far better coaching atmosphere for ministering to the dying.

What Happens After They Die

On the mind of almost every dying person is the question, "What will happen to me after I die?" Even those who were never part of a church and were never interested in spiritual things begin to ask themselves spiritual questions when they know they are dying. The question of an afterlife and what the requirements are for getting there become a pressing reality.

My experience shows that not only do most dying people think about this, but 99% of them want to talk about it. They want to settle this issue before it is too late. There are the rare exceptions who do not want to discuss their eternal destiny. They are content not knowing. Most individuals, however, want to talk about what is going to happen to them. I find individuals falling into one of three camps:

1. Their eternal destiny is settled. They are confident about what will happen to them after they die. These individuals usually face death with a great amount of confidence and peace.

2. They hope they will go to "heaven," but they are not positive that they will. They also are not sure what the requirements are to get there. Many of these individuals are scared, knowing this issue is not settled within them.

3. They are pretty sure their eternal destiny is not going to be pleasant. They have lived a rebellious life, and now are fearful about the consequences they will reap from their actions. Many of these individuals show great signs of agitation and unrest as they approach end of life.

The goal of the end-of-life coach is not to step in and force his view of the afterlife upon the dying. Besides being the opposite of a coach approach, it usually does no good. My experience has shown that when I approach a coachee with my agenda in the foreground, wanting to push my views upon them, they want nothing to do with me. They ask me not to come back, or refuse to go deep with me. They no longer feel safe.

A coach will always meet the dying where they are. Love them just as they are. Get to know them. Affirm them. Show interest in their life. When this is done and the dying feel safe (back to supporting building block #1), they will begin going deep with you. When they know they are safe and grasp that they are loved just as they are, the dying make the connection that perhaps God (whom you represent) just might love them and accept them in the same way. That's when the spiritual questions begin to be asked.

A powerful question that can be helpful is to simply ask, "What is going to happen to you after you die?" The coachee's response will indicate not only what camp he falls in, but how he is feeling about it, and whether or not this is something he wants to discuss in preparation for his death.

When the dying are uncertain about their eternal destiny and don't know the "requirements" to get to Heaven, the coach can clarify. Permission should always be asked first. For example, "Would you like me to share with you what the Bible says about how a person can get to heaven?" My experience has been that the answer to that question is almost always "YES!" The dying are begging me to tell them the answer to the question that has been plaguing them. At this point the clergy can share with their parishioners, according to their faith tradition, how one can be confident about their eternal destiny.

Having this issue settled makes such a difference. There are many illustrations of this that I could recite, but I will share just one. I went to visit a brand new hospice patient, a man I will call Bob. When I arrived at his home, Bob was agitated and struggling to breathe. He was wearing oxygen, but it was obviously not helping him. I called our nurse, and she was on her way. In between breaths, I talked with Bob. I asked him what he was thinking about. Bob told me how scared he was to die. "Tell me more," I said. Bob went on to tell me about the rotten, selfish life that he had lived. Now, as he stared death in the face, he regretted his past, but said it was too late. He felt hopeless and anticipated great pain and agony ahead for him. He told me how he had denied God and mocked Christians all his life. Now he was ready to stand before God, and the thought terrified him. He asked me, "Is there any help for me? Is there any way I can make it right with God?" I asked him if he would like for me to share with him what the Bible says about being forgiven and about how one can go to heaven. In his pain and great struggle to breathe he begged me to tell him.

Coming from an evangelical Christian background, I shared with him about God's love and His desire to be Bob's friend. I told him about Jesus and how he died on the cross to pay the penalty for our sin, and rose from the dead to purchase that place for us in heaven, which he offers as a free gift. I explained to Bob that if he believed and accepted that, and wanted those gifts of forgiveness and eternal life in heaven, all he had to do was to talk to God about it. Bob asked me to help him and we prayed together. When we finished praying, Bob laid his head down, and I noticed he was breathing more easily. I asked Bob how he was doing. He told me that he had never felt such peace, and that for the first time he was not afraid to die. He lay silently for a few moments with his eyes closed, breathing peacefully, and then he reached his arms up into the air above him. I said, "Bob. What are you doing?" He said, "It's Jesus. He is right here with me. Everything will be OK." Then he brought his arms down and crossed them onto his chest, as though he were pulling someone in close to him. The family members present couldn't believe the change – physically, emotionally, and spiritually. Bob now had hope, and it made all the difference in the world. Bob died later that evening—a calm, peaceful death without struggle.

I could recite story after story of dying coachees who expressed to me their pain and struggle because they knew they were dying, and they had not yet settled the question of their eternal destiny. A few of these individuals chose not to talk about it further. That was their choice. Coaching is all about the coachee and their wishes. Most, however, wanted nothing more than to settle the burning struggle within them, and were looking for someone who would hear them out and help them work through their struggle. This is one of the great privileges of the end-of-life coach.

Peaceful Death with Dignity

When the dying get to the point where they are nearing their final breath, they are usually ready to let go. They are tired of their pain and discomfort. They have made their peace on earth. And they have completed their preparations for their eternal destiny. My experience shows that, for them, death is a welcome release. When they finally surrender to the moment and let go, I imagine there to be an incredible experience of liberation. There must be a free-at-last kind of ecstasy from all the constraints and bondage that go along with being trapped in the human body.

The family of the dying, however, do not usually experience the same free-at-last ecstasy. For them the hard work of grief and mourning is just beginning. (The second half of this book will focus on using a coach approach to minister to these grieving individuals.)

Nonetheless, what the family has experienced is something special and meaningful. They have had the privilege of walking their loved one to the door of eternity. Think of it this way: When an individual or family invites people to their home for dinner, the evening usually ends in a typical way. Rarely does the host sit in his living room and say, "Thank you for coming. Have a safe ride home. Good night." Rather the host gets up out of his chair and walks his company to the door and, from there, bids them farewell. That shows respect. It shows appreciation for the time spent together. It is a sincere way to say goodbye. What the family of your dead coachee has done is to walk their loved one to the door of eternity. Sharing their loved one's journey to this door is the last gift the family gives to the dying one. Although it is difficult to see at the time because of the intense shock and the grief, it is an amazing spiritual experience. The end-of-life coach who is able to experience this with the family is privileged.

Chapter Eight

Coaching the Grieving

I write these words after returning home from facilitating a grief support group. One of the group members entered the meeting room in tears. After inquiring about the tears, the group members and I learned that this woman had just completed a session with her grief counselor. She was upset because her counselor told her that it was approaching two years since her husband of 62 years had died and that she should be over it by now. He told her to come back next week, where he would begin the process of getting her fixed up.

In my opinion, this woman did not need to see a counselor; she needed an end-of-life coach. She did not need to be "fixed." She needed someone to walk the journey of grief with her.

How does the end-of-life coach go about doing that? How does one coach the grieving?

As with coaching the dying, the place to start is by remembering "The Eight Building Blocks." They must provide the framework for our coaching.

The Eight Supporting Building Blocks for Coaching the Grieving

Keeping in mind the eight building blocks, I now want to add eight supporting building blocks for coaching the grieving.

1) Provide A Safe Place

Supporting building block #1 is the same for coaching the dying and the grieving. When it comes to the grieving, however, it is even more important. Because of the culture in which we live, most people do not understand the journey of grief. Beyond not understanding it, many are uncomfortable being around a person who is grieving. People don't know how to respond to a grieving person. Because THEY are uncomfortable, they push the grieving person to "get over" their grief and criticize them when they do their work of mourning. The result is a country filled with grieving people who do not feel understood or supported in their grief. Taking it a step further, because many have found disapproval for their method of grieving, they have learned to keep to themselves and not share with anyone. "It's just not safe," they say.

Grief produces a wide range of normal emotions. Some of the typical emotions a grieving person experiences are shock, sadness, anxiety, guilt, hopelessness, fear, disorganization, confusion, anger, hatred, jealousy, joy and relief, just to name a few. These emotions are not always the easiest to deal with.

The picture below is what H. Norman Wright calls the "Tangled Ball of Emotions." It shows what the emotions of grief are like for many people. There are many different emotions that are commonly experienced—sometimes all at the same time. They are all tangled and mixed together, at times making it difficult to sort out the emotions being experienced. The emotions are unpredictable—the griever can feel fine one moment and then, all of a sudden, be crying uncontrollably. Sometimes the emotions feel overwhelming, and sometimes out of control.

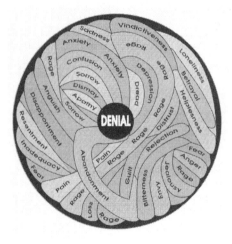

Reprinted with permission. (Wright 2006, 64).

Right in the center of this circle is denial. This is the initial emotion that most individuals experience when they hear the news of the death of a loved one. They feel shock, numbness and disbelief. There is the feeling of being dazed or stunned. I believe these feelings are gifts from God. They temporarily, psychologically protect those who learn of a loved one's death, until they are more able to tolerate what they don't want to believe. They are a temporary time-out, until we are able to face the full reality of the death. I sometimes describe denial as a "natural injection of anesthesia." Especially in the beginning of the grief journey, one's emotions need time to catch up with what their mind has been told. I believe that if we were hit with all the feelings of grief at one time, we would not be able to survive it. Then, after the initial denial, one by one we can face all the emotions above and accept the reality of the death. That's when the hard work of grieving begins and where the emotions can easily get out of control.

It is easy to see why many are uncomfortable with someone who is grieving. It is understandable that family and friends will try to get their loved ones "over" their grief, and to stop them when they openly express these emotions. But it is equally clear and understandable that, as a result, those in the midst of grief do not feel safe in sharing with many people.

Hence, when you coach the grieving, provide a safe place. The individual in mourning needs to know they can openly mourn their loss in their own way. Coaching is all about the coachee. They set the agenda. They select the intensity. This is why those in grief need a coach.

How does one go about providing this safe place for their grieving coachees?

Before I answer that question in the sections below, let me begin with this caveat: Although all of the grief reactions below are normal and expected, if they continue for an extended period of time without change, or if the grieving individual brings harm to themselves or others, or threatens to do so, a referral to a mental health professional should be made.

Allow Them to Hurt

One of the most difficult tasks in coaching the grieving is allowing them to hurt. Grief hurts. Attendees of my grief support groups regularly comment on the fact that grief is far more painful than they could ever have imagined. The normal tendency when someone is hurting is to want to make them feel better. The end-of-life coach will refrain from doing this. As a matter of fact, it will be common for the end result of time spent with a grief coach to be that the coachee feels worse. This can mean that the session went well. It was stated earlier that loss has to be grieved and mourned. The pain needs to be faced head on. The intense feelings need to be embraced. The only way to move beyond the feelings of grief is to walk through them. The effective end-of-life coach will sit with his coachees in their pain, not try to remove the pain. He will walk the journey of suffering with them, not tell them they need to be strong or buck it up or keep busy. If a coach gives in to the natural instinct to try to remove the hurt, he will most likely remove the opportunity for real healing to occur. In addition, he will subconsciously be sending the message to his coachees that hurting is wrong, and that if they are going to hurt, this is not a safe place for them to do so.

Allow Them to Cry

On the heels of "allow them to hurt" is "allow them to cry." We already stated that crying is a good, healthy outlet for our pain. Crying is a form of mourning. Once again, the natural instinct when someone in your presence begins to cry is to try to make them feel better. We rush over to give them a hug. We hand them a tissue. There are times when these gestures are appreciated by the coachee. More often than not, however, the message received when a coachee is hugged or handed a tissue is, "Wipe those tears. It's time to stop crying. I want to lessen your pain." A better response might be for the coach to say, "I love your tears. Go ahead and cry if you want. Tears are wonderful. If you want a tissue, there are some over here, but feel free to let the tears flow." And when the coachee has stopped crying and is again able to speak, the coach can say something like, "Tell me about the tears …" That is what it means to provide a safe, healing place which is all about the coachee.

Permission to Feel Whatever They Feel

A safe place is a place where the coachee can feel whatever he feels without being told that he "shouldn't feel that way," or that "he needs to get over it or deal with it," or that "what he is feeling is not a very godly feeling," or that "he needs to stop because he is not being a good testimony to others." These are comments that I hear being spoken all the time. The result is always the same. The grieving learn that "this is not a safe place where I can be real."

As stated above, the grieving will feel some intense emotions. They need a safe place to get them out. The anger they might feel (which is their form of protest, saying "This is not what I wanted to happen!") might be directed toward a doctor, or toward their loved one, or toward God, or even toward their coach, or their spiritual leader.

I was the end-of-life coach for a man who was dying. Prior to his death, I met with this man in the afternoon. His wife told me, "You need to tell John that he must get better. You must pray that God will spare him. I am not ready to lose my husband." Later that evening I received news that John had died, and I was asked to come to the house. When I arrived, the wife ran toward me and literally started punching me, while yelling, "You didn't do your job. You were supposed to tell him to stay alive." She wasn't really angry with me, but there was a lot of anger inside that needed to be let out. I was that safe place where she could do so. In the months to come, I was able to walk the journey of grief with her, and she felt safe to be real and to be herself.

Below are a few things to remember about emotions which could be helpful to your coachees:

- You are not your emotions. Your emotions and feelings come and go.

- Feelings aren't good or bad, they just are.

- It's okay to feel sad and cry. Jesus cried when His friend died (John 11:35).

- It's okay to feel anger. Many of the prophets of the Bible, and even Jesus, felt angry.

- It's okay to feel happy, laugh, and have fun. You can't be sad all the time, and sometimes you just need to get your mind off the work of grieving and have fun with friends.

- It's okay to feel guilty. You may have had a fight with the person who died or wished that person dead. Your wishing cannot kill anybody. Maybe you wished you had spent more time with the person or done what they asked you to do. If you are having a hard time with feelings of this kind, talk to your coach, or try writing a letter to the person who died.

- It's okay to feel afraid. You may be afraid because you're not sure who will take care of you, or where the money will come from, or if you'll have enough money for clothes or food. Sit down with your coach or a trusted adult and discuss your concerns.

- It's okay to feel these feelings in your body. God built our bodies to handle stress.

- You may find that you actually feel relieved if a death ends a long illness or other difficult situation. This feeling can be hard to admit, but it's normal.

- It's okay to feel disorganized or panicked. You may even experience anxiety attacks. These usually pass, but they are uncomfortable.

- It's okay to not feel anything. You may go out with friends, laugh, and have fun after you hear about a death. It's one way your emotional self protects itself from a big shock.

Permission to Say Whatever They Want to Say

Because of the intense emotions, grieving people sometimes say things that would not normally be acceptable things to say. They might verbalize extreme anger toward other individuals or toward God. In normal situations, a person like this might be asked to "watch his mouth" or "not speak that way." When coaching an individual in grief, however, the coach would do well to listen intently as this individual talks, encouraging them to share more. This will enable the coachee to release what they are feeling. In this situation, it is not only acceptable, but it is healthy.

The person in grief might say that they have no hope to go on, that life is now without meaning or that they wish their life was over. In a normal situation, the person who says these words would need to be placed on a suicide watch, and professional help would need to be sought immediately. Most grieving people who say these words, however, have no intention of killing themselves. They are simply saying, "This is how badly I hurt," and "This is how much I am going to miss my loved one." This individual still needs to be questioned to make sure they do not have plans to harm themselves. Talk of suicide always needs to be taken seriously. What the grieving need more than anything, however, is to know that you are a safe enough place for them to share even this deepest feeling and pain. I would probably respond to this grieving individual by saying something like, "It sounds like you are really hurting. Tell me more about the pain you are feeling." Or, "To actually bring harm to yourself is not acceptable behavior, but it sure makes sense that you would be hurting badly enough to say these things. Share with me more of what is going on with you now."

The grieving individual does not need someone to correct the things he is saying, nor does he need someone to try to change his thinking to be more positive. He needs a coach who will sit with him and allow him to say whatever he needs to say as he processes the many emotions he is experiencing. And if you allow him to speak even these explosive words, you will be providing a safe place where he can feel safe enough to go deep with you.

There are times when your coachee might not want to say anything. Don't press him. Remember that he is in charge. Be comfortable to sit with him in silence. Giving your coachee times of silence might be a gift. Mourning requires periods of silence and solitude. Many who don't understand the grief journey, or who want to step in and fix the one grieving, will not allow for this needed silence. Silence is also helpful for the coach. It reminds him of the priority of listening over speaking, making their coachee's needs primary. It reminds him of the intensity of the emotions that are present—within the coachee, as well as his own feelings. It reminds him of the fact that the mystery of grief is such that words are often inadequate. Silence helps to create a safe place for the one grieving.

Permission to Do Whatever They Want to Do

Coaching an individual in grief means that the time together is all about the coachee. The coachee has the freedom to feel anything without being told he shouldn't feel that way. He may say anything he needs to say, in expressing his pain and loss. Keeping in mind the caveat previously mentioned in this chapter regarding referrals to a mental health professional where appropriate, the next step in this progression is that the grieving individual is permitted to do whatever they want to do.

A long-time member of my church recently died. His wife, Mary, a devout Christian, was grieving appropriately. She was crying and mourning her loss. She was lonely and missed her husband terribly. A few weeks into her grief, some of her friends came to me, worried about Mary. Mary told them she didn't want to come to church anymore. She hurt too badly and just wanted to stay home. I asked what they told her. The friends told Mary she was not permitted to stay home. She needed to be in church and she needed to be surrounded by other people. But things only got worse for Mary, and she threatened all the more to stay home. The friends asked me to talk to her and to convince her she must continue to attend church. I told them I would talk to her, but that I was going to give her permission to stay home, and that they needed to give her the same permission. Mary stayed home for two Sundays and then returned, saying church is where she wanted to be. But Mary needed to figure that out for herself. The only way she could do that was to have the freedom to stay home.

Some will clean out their loved one's clothes right away, while others will wait a long time to do so. Some will attend a support group, while others will spend long periods of time alone. Some will visit their doctor to get medication to help them face their grief, while others will refuse any form of medication. As long as they are doing their work of mourning, the grieving need to be permitted to grieve in their own way, and to do whatever they want to do. The coach who allows the grieving to choose their own path, supporting them wherever they are, will be providing a safe place where ministry can take place.

Don't Try to Fix Them

I have said this all along, but I will say it again. Those who are in the midst of grief do not need to be fixed. The more they are mourning and letting out their grief, especially initially, the better they are doing. What they do need, however, is a coach to walk the journey with them. But in order for the coach to be able to make a difference, he has to establish a safe place, where the coachee can be real and can face his grief head on.

2) Ride the Roller Coaster with Them

The second supporting building block for coaching the grieving, like with coaching the dying, is to be present with them. Here, however, it is labeled differently. Being present with the grieving is anything but static. Rather than being still with them, most of the time is spent moving quickly to keep up with them. Instead of the image of being present by the bedside of the dying, this image is boarding a roller coaster with the grieving, and going for the ride of your life with them.

I know no better picture to describe the journey of grief than a roller coaster. There are times of being at great heights, followed by steep drops of emotions to the very bottom. The ups and downs continue, often at unexpected intervals. At the same time, grief does not follow a direct route. There are twists and turns, and times when life turns completely upside down. It comes to a sudden stop, and then starts all over again. Thus describes the journey of grief.

What the grieving need more than anything else is someone to ride the roller coaster with them. They don't need someone to tell them when to get on or off. They don't need someone to give riding instructions. They don't need correction as to how to ride better; they need a companion along the journey.

This was driven home very clearly to me in my early years of pastoral ministry. Some members of my congregation died. I ministered to these families and offered what I thought were some great, insightful instructions to help them deal with their grief. (I now realize that I probably greatly annoyed them.) Then I received a call that the teen-age daughter of a family was dead. I went to the house and sat with the family for hours. I was so distraught by what happened, I didn't know what to say. I gave no instructions. I offered no advice. I simply sat with the family in silence, crying with them. After many hours, I got up and left. I felt like the worst, most ineffective pastor in the world. I drove home beating myself up, feeling like a total failure. I thought I had been totally useless to this family. Yet in the days to come, I was told over and over what an incredible help I had been. They could not thank me enough for ministering to them so effectively. I thought, "What???? I did nothing but sit there with them." That was exactly what they needed. They didn't need my wise words of instruction. They needed for me to be present. They needed for me to ride the roller coaster with them.

Expected and Unexpected Friends

It is often surprising for the individual in grief to see who will ride the roller coaster with them and who will not. Often those whom they expect to board the coaster with them are never seen again. Some whom they thought would never be present become their closest companions.

I share this because the expected and unexpected friend issue often becomes one that is heavy on the heart of the grieving. The refusal of expected friends to be present can be a secondary grief issue. The coach will want to be sensitive to this and take note of the available support. Helpful, powerful questions to be asked are: "Tell me about your support system," or "In addition to me, who has come along side to walk this journey of grief with you?"

Work Through Your Own Grief Issues

Before you can truly be present with a grieving coachee, you must work through your own issues related to grief. The process for doing that will be described in more detail in chapter 11, "The End-of-Life Coach." For now, it is enough to say that until you work through your own personal issues, you will never be able to be truly present with the grieving. Your focus will always be on yourself, your feelings, your reactions, your fears and your experiences of loss. How freeing, both for you and your coachee, when you can be truly present with them. That's when real ministry takes place!

What Not to Say

As the end-of-life coach rides the roller coaster with his grieving coachees, there are some comments and phrases he will want to avoid using. Chapter 3 of this book lists some common clichés that should be avoided. They bring to the grieving a sense of frustration and a need to be defensive. The coach who uses these clichés will appear to be insensitive rather than supportive. Allow me to highlight a few of them, and to give some additional tips on things not to say to the grieving.

Don't Say You Understand

- I know what you are feeling.
- I went through the exact same thing.

Avoid Beginning Any Sentence with "At Least. . . ."

- At least you had a good life with her.

- At least he's in heaven now.

- At least you have two other children.

- At least you are young and can get married again.

- At least you didn't have to go through the pain of birth.

Avoid Trying to Explain What God Is Doing Behind the Scenes.

- God is making you stronger through this.

- This baby must just have not been meant to be.

- It is all part of God's plan.

- Cancer is a gift from God because you are so strong.

Avoid Attempts to Minimize Your Coachee's Pain.

- Be happy. He's no longer suffering and is in a better place.

- It's okay, you can have other children.

- Be glad that he died at an early age. He doesn't have to experience pain and heartache on this earth.

Avoid Comparing What Your Coachee Is Going Through to ANYTHING Else or Anyone Else's Problem.

- It's not as bad as that time I …

- My brother lost his wife and his son on the same day.

Don't Blame Your Coachee.

- If you had more faith, she would have been healed.

- You are not praying hard enough.

- Maybe God is punishing you. Have you done something sinful?

- Oh, you're not going to let this get you down, are you?

Don't Make Your Coachee Feel Guilty for Mourning.

- Are you still not over this?

- You know she wouldn't have wanted you to feel this way.

Avoid Using Statements that Begin with "You Should" or "You Will."

- You should be glad she is out of pain.

- You should take up a hobby.

- You will feel better soon.

Don't Offer Your Grieving Coachee Spiritual Answers, at Least Not Initially.

- This is sent for your own good, and you need to embrace it to get all the benefit out of it.

- Remember that God is in control.

- Remember, all things work together for good, for those that love God and are called according to His purpose.

Don't Place a Timetable on Their Recovery.

- Give it a week and you will forget about him.

- Time will heal all wounds.

What to Say

See section 3 below.

3) Invite Them to Tell Their Story

The third supporting building block for coaching the grieving focuses on what is useful to say to our coachees. One of the best, most helpful things we can say to them is, "Tell me your story." Most of those in grief love to tell their story. They need to tell their story. Telling one's story is a big part of the process of mourning on the path toward healing. It is a way they acknowledge the reality of their loss. It allows them to recognize and admit their emotions and pain. It is an important way that they look back in order to remember and to hold onto memories. It is a wonderful step in their process of looking forward in the hope of discovering renewed meaning and purpose.

As important as it is for the grieving to tell their stories, there are not many people who will give them that opportunity. The telling of their story takes time. In our fast-paced society, many don't want to give up that time. The telling of their story takes someone with a receptive spirit. The grieving will often go on and on about the minute details of their loved one's sickness or death. They will share far more than you needed or ever wanted to hear. But it's not all about you and what you need. It is about the grieving one who is sharing and his needs. Yet many will get frustrated quickly. The hearing of their story takes patience. The grieving one may very well share the same story over and over again. Each time they tell it, it is as if it is brand new. They need to do this. Repeating the story is a way of processing and accepting the death. Not everyone has the patience to listen to the same story over and over. As a result, many have no one to listen to their story. This greatly affects those who are grieving and blocks their progress toward healing.

As an end-of-life coach, it is crucial that you not only listen to your grieving coachee's story, but that you invite him to share it. All the basic coaching building blocks come into play here—your deep listening, your coaching relationship, powerful questions, artful language, creating awareness. You are inviting them to tell you more, and more, and more. The grieving will be able to tell if you are a compassionate listener and if you are being attentive to their story. If you are, you will be providing a ministry to your coachees beyond what words can describe.

What will be included in their stories?

Memories

One of the things your coachee will likely include in their story is memories of times spent with their loved one. They are thinking of these memories constantly. So when it seems like they have an endless supply of those memories ready to share, they probably do! And again, they need to share them. Listen. Engage. Invite.

I remind my coachees that these memories are precious gifts from God which no one can take away. They are theirs to hold onto forever. I encourage my coachees to keep their loved one alive by sharing them.

On a practical note for clergy, it is in listening to these memories that a lot of information for the funeral can be gathered. By inviting them to share, you are getting the personal information you need, while at the same time helping them in their grief journey.

Relationship

Most likely, your coachee will also include detailed information about the relationship they shared with their loved one who died. This will include strengths about their relationship, as well as things they wish had been different. Most of the time, your coachee will not need for you to comment on their relationship. Remember, you are not there to fix them. You are there to walk the grief journey with them. They definitely do not need you to smooth over the areas of weakness, saying, "Oh, it wasn't that bad. You did fine." They need you to listen and affirm that you have heard. They need the opportunity to work through their own feelings of guilt and regret, to come to their own conclusion that they had done their best, or to grant themselves forgiveness if they had failed. All of that comes through in the sharing of their story. And the only way they will come to peace within themselves is if they come to their own resolution about these issues.

Details

Your coachee will probably share with you in great detail the circumstances surrounding their loved one's death—the illness, the tragedy, what led up to the death, what the last day was like, what the last hour was like, what the last seconds were like, what your coachee did during this time, what happened immediately following the death, who was present, who was not present, the last words their loved one spoke, the words spoken by everyone else in the room, where their loved one is now, and what they are experiencing. Every detail is needed in enabling them to come to grips with the reality of their loved one's death, and to reconcile it into their own life. There is a good chance that they will tell you these details numerous times—perhaps every time you meet with them. Because this is all about them and not the coach, the coach will refrain from stopping the sharing and saying, "You already told me this!" Even though the coach will be thinking this, he must remember that sharing the story is what will most benefit the coachee. He will listen attentively and encourage his coachees to share even more.

Emotions

"What are you feeling?" is a powerful question to ask your grieving coachees. Their answer will get them sharing this part of their story. Before they can work through the many emotions of grief, they have to be aware of the ones they are experiencing. The end-of-life coach can help his coachees to identify these emotions, to label them, to normalize their existence, and then to walk through each of the emotions with them. Most grieving individuals have within themselves all they need to work through these emotions and come to resolution about them. The end-of-life coach will help them to move forward in this process of discovery.

Fears and Struggles

One additional area that will in all likelihood be included in your grieving coachee's stories is their fears and struggles. This will include physical, emotional, spiritual, financial, relational, and other practical fears and struggles. Describing these fears and struggles in detail is not necessary in this textbook. What is important for the coach to remember is that the grieving are usually not looking for you to solve or alleviate them. They are looking for you to listen as they share their story. They want to know that you will not be scared away by their fears. They want the assurance that you will walk through their struggles with them. The sharing of their fears and struggles is part of their mourning.

When some time has passed and the coachee has been doing his work of mourning, he might revisit these fears and struggles. This time, answers and solutions may be desired. This is when the coach will use his coaching expertise to help his coachees to discover their own solutions. Empowering them in this way will be another step forward in their healing.

Don't Use Euphemisms

One final practical note in this supporting building block is that, when a coach invites his coachees to tell their story, he must be mindful not to use euphemisms for death. One of the purposes of sharing their story is that it helps the storytellers face the reality of their loved one's death. If the coach refers to the deceased as one who expired or passed away, he is masking the reality. The coach helps his coachee when he gently and compassionately acknowledges that his coachee's loved one has "died" and is now "dead".

4) Assure Them with What Is Normal

Having spent years coaching the grieving and hundreds of hours leading grief support groups, there is one question that mourners have asked me far above any other question. That question is "Am I going crazy?" The second most common question is "Am I normal?"

The journey through grief can be so radically different from our everyday realities that sometimes it feels more like being picked up and dropped onto the surface of the moon than it does a journey through earth. What is unusual in life is often usual in grief. Because we live in a culture that doesn't talk openly about death and grief, however, most individuals in grief do not know that what they are experiencing is normal. As a matter of fact, they fear just the opposite.

Therefore, one of the greatest and most needed takeaways for someone in the midst of grief is the realization that what they are going through is normal.

On a regular occurrence, I will have people come to me who have been referred by their doctor. The doctor tells them that they need therapy. They need to see a grief counselor. Their grief is affecting their everyday behavior and their overall health. They are told they are in need of counseling. Nine times out of ten, these individuals don't need a grief counselor. They need a grief coach to walk alongside of them. They have one primary fact that they need to learn. They need to be told that what they are experiencing is normal. They are not going crazy. Hearing and understanding those simple words allows them to walk away from my office as a new person. Now, instead of panicking that something is majorly wrong, they feel free to do the work of mourning, with the support of a coach who will walk the journey of grief with them.

The International Coach Federation lists the "Top Ten Indicators to Refer a Client to a Mental Health Professional." They are as follows:

Your client …

1. Is exhibiting a decline in his/her ability to experience pleasure and/or an increase in being sad, hopeless and helpless.

    −   As a coach, you may notice that your client is not as upbeat as usual.

    −   He/she may talk much more frequently about how awful life/the world is and that nothing can be done about it.

    −   The client may make comments about "why bother" or "what's the use."

    −   There will be a decline in talking about things that are enjoyable.

    −   He/she may stop doing things they like to do (examples: going to the movies, visiting with friends, participating in athletic events or being a spectator of sporting events).

    −   The client begins to talk about being unable to do anything that forwards their dreams or desires.

2. Has intrusive thoughts or is unable to concentrate or focus.

    −   As a coach, you may notice that your client is not able to focus on their goals or the topic of conversation.

    −   The client is unable to complete their action steps and isn't aware of what got in the way.

    −   You notice that your client begins talking about unpleasant events during the course of talking about themselves and their goals.

    −   The client tells you that unpleasant thoughts keep popping into their minds at inopportune moments, or when they are thinking about or doing other things, and that they can't seem to get away from these thoughts.

    −   Your client tells you about recurring scary dreams that they didn't have before.

    −   Your client reports that they have so many thoughts swirling in their heads and that they can't get them to slow down.

3. Is unable to get to sleep or awakens during the night and is unable to get back to sleep, or sleeps excessively.

    -   Your client comes to his/her coaching sessions tired and exhausted.

    -   Your client begins talking about not being able to get to sleep or how he/she just wants to sleep all the time.

    -   Your client may report to you how he/she gets to sleep and then wakes up and can't get back to sleep.

    -   Your client tells you how he/she needs to take naps during the day, something they have not done before.

    -   Your client reports that they fell asleep at an inopportune time or place.

4. Has a change in appetite: decrease in appetite or increase in appetite.

    -   Your client reports that he/she isn't hungry and just doesn't want to eat.

    -   Your client reports that he/she is eating all the time, usually sweets or junk food, whether or not they are hungry.

    -   Your client says he/she doesn't get any enjoyment from eating, when they did in the past.

    -   Your client reports that he/she is not sitting down to eat with friends or family, when he/she did in the past.

5. Is feeling guilty because others have suffered or died.

    -   Your client reports that he/she feels guilty because they are alive or have not been injured.

    -   Your client states that he/she doesn't understand why he/she is still here/alive when others have had to suffer/die.

    -   Your client doesn't want to move forward with his/her goals because he/she doesn't deserve to have the life he/she chose, especially when other people have had to suffer/die.

    -   Your client questions his/her right to have a fulfilling life/career in the face of all that has happened.

    -   Your client expresses the belief that he/she is unworthy of having a satisfying life.

6. Has feelings of despair or hopelessness.

- According to your client nothing in life is OK.
- Your client misses session times or says he/she wants to quit coaching, because life is not worth living or he/she doesn't deserve to get what they want.
- Your client moves into excessive negative thinking.
- Your client says that he/she can't make a difference or that whatever he/she does doesn't matter.
- Your client has the attitude of "Why bother?"

7. Is hyper alert and/or excessively tired.

   - Your client reports that he/she can't relax.
   - Your client states that he/she is jumping at the slightest noise.
   - Your client reports that it feels like she/he always has to be on guard.
   - Your client states that they are listening for any little sound that is out of the ordinary.
   - Your client reports that he/she has no energy.
   - Your client states that he/she can't do their usual chores because he/she is so tired.
   - Your client states that it takes too much energy to do things he/she normally did in the past.

8. Has increased irritability or outbursts of anger.

   - Your client becomes increasingly belligerent or argumentative with you or other people.
   - Your client reports that everyone or everything annoys them.
   - Your client starts making comments about how miserable everyone and everything is.
   - Your client reports that other people in their life are telling them how miserable/angry they have become.
   - Your client reports getting into arguments with people.
   - Your client states that they get so upset they don't know what to do with themselves.
   - Your client reports that they feel like a "pressure cooker" or are "ready to burst."

- Your client increasingly tells you about doing things or wanting to do things that would harm themselves or others (examples: wanting to put their fist through a window; wanting to punch someone; wanting to hit someone/something with their car).

9. Has impulsive and risk-taking behavior.

   - Your client reports doing things, such as going on a buying spree, without thinking about the consequences of their behavior.

   - Your client tells you that something came to their mind, so they went and did it without thinking about the outcome.

   - Your client reports an increase in doing things that could be detrimental to themselves or others (examples: increase in promiscuous sexual behavior; increase in alcohol/drug consumption; deciding to get married after knowing someone an unusually short period of time).

10. Has thoughts of death and/or suicide.

    - Your client begins talking a lot about death, not just a fear of dying.

    - Your client alludes to the fact that dying would be appropriate for them.

    - Your client makes comments that to die right now would be OK with them.

    - Your client becomes fascinated with what dying would be like.

    - Your client talks about ways to die.

    - Your client talks about going to a better place and how wonderful it would be, and seems to be carried away by the thought.

    - Your client tells you they know how they would kill themselves if they wanted to/had the chance.

    - Your client alludes to having a plan or way they would die/go to a better place/ leave the planet/leave the situation/get out of here.

    - Whereas previously your client was engaging, personable and warm, and now they present to you as cold, distant and aloof, tell them what you are observing and ask them what has changed for them. This is often a signal that they have disengaged from living and are silently thinking or planning to commit suicide.

Prepared by: Lynn F. Meinke, MA, RN, CLC, CSLC, Life Coach

When the average coachee exhibits any of these behaviors, especially if they exhibit a number of these behaviors at the same time, it is an indication that something is wrong. These individuals should be referred to a mental health professional. All ten of these behaviors, however, are absolutely normal for someone who is grieving. No wonder the grieving think they are going crazy. Add to this all the extreme emotions that an individual in grief experiences and you can see why one might think they need therapy. Everyone around them, who does not understand grief, thinks they are in need of therapy too!

Not only is grief emotional, grief is also physical. In the myths of grief listed earlier, myth #6 was "Grief is only an emotional reaction." Those who buy into this myth, then experience the normal physical symptoms of grief, think they are going crazy.

The reality is, grieving is hard work. It is physically abusive, mentally demanding and spiritually challenging. I can't think of any other work that I have done that can compare to its intensity or its impact. The exhaustion from grieving is similar to a heavy physical workout.

Below are some common "symptoms" of grieving which are sometimes mistakenly diagnosed as strictly physical problems:

- Chest pains or heart problems
- Dizziness
- Dry mouth
- Empty feeling in the stomach
- Fatigue
- Feeling of "something stuck in the throat"
- Headache
- Inability to sleep
- Sleeping all the time
- Loss of sexual desire or having overly active sexual desire
- Loss of weight or gaining weight
- Nausea and vomiting
- Increased allergic reactions

- Oversensitivity to noise

- Purposeless activity

- Hyperactivity

- Shortness of breath

- Trembling

- Uncontrollable sighing and sobbing

- Weakness in the muscles

- Various gastrointestinal symptoms: constipation, diarrhea, or excessive gas

Any of these symptoms can be a normal part of the grieving process. If they persist or become very uncomfortable, your coachee should make an appointment with his health care provider and tell him/her that he has experienced a recent major loss.

Some people find themselves relating to the physical symptoms of the loved one who died, which again makes them think they are going crazy. For example, if their loved one died from a brain tumor, they may have more frequent headaches; if from a heart attack, they may have chest pains. This sometimes becomes an unconscious way of identifying with and feeling close to that person. It is another one of the ways our bodies might respond to our loss.

The grieving individual often does not feel in control of how his body is responding. Your coachee's body might be communicating with him about the stress he is experiencing. This is not a sign of going crazy. In the majority of instances, the physical symptoms described above are normal and temporary.

Many who come for grief coaching will do so because they don't understand all of this. They are exhibiting normal behavior and don't know it! The end-of-life coach will do well to keep this building block in mind every time he meets with a grieving coachee.

5) Give Them the Time That They Need

Today's fast-paced society encourages, and even demands, that we live efficiently. In the proverbial blink of an eye, modern technology makes it possible for us to complete tasks that took previous generations days or weeks. Unfortunately, this has given our generation a "microwave mentality." We want what we want, and we want it now! Look around you. There is a fast, quick, instant, speedy service for just about anything you can think of, including espressos, fast food, medical checkups and oil changes. Our society has forgotten that quality takes time. We have become impatient. You know the type—the guy that repeatedly punches the elevator call button because it will make the car arrive faster.

Many take this microwave mentality and apply it to the journey of grief. They want it to be quick. They want it done and over with so they can move on with their life. As I was writing these words, I received a phone call from a man who was part of my Hospice Bereavement Follow Up program. His father died three months ago and, as per practice, I follow up with the bereaved with cards, letters, a monthly newsletter, phone calls, etc. This man called to ask that he be removed from the mailing list. His exact words were, "I need to be removed from that list. It's been three months. It is long enough. I would rather not be reminded any more. I would like to just move on." I honored this man's request, but I was concerned about him. The journey of grief cannot be rushed. "Not being reminded" is not a healthy way of dealing with grief. Facing the grief and doing the work of mourning is what is needed. The end-of-life coach should be aware that some will try to rush their grief experience.

The more common issue the end-of-life coach will face is not that his coachee is trying to rush his grief, but rather that others are encouraging him to do so. People who have not experienced a major loss themselves have a greater chance of buying into the microwave mentality of grief. They expect others to "get over it" quickly. They will push them to do so. One of the most painful, yet oft spoken, phrases to an individual in grief is, "Aren't you over it yet?"

The end-of-life coach must be aware of this and give his coachee all the time that he needs. The journey of grief is anything but a quick trip. For most people, it is a slow journey which never completely ends. We never forget. (This is a person we have loved. We don't want to forget!) Most of our coachees will continue to grieve for the rest of their lives. Her grief should not continue at the initial intensity. She should learn how to integrate this grief into her life. Yet, it will still be present and, at times, painful.

There is no time table for getting over grief. There are, however, different time periods in the grief journey that are more difficult than others. The end-of-life coach should be aware of these.

The First Year

The whole first year of the grief journey is difficult. The one grieving must not only adjust to not having their loved one physically present with them, but they will experience many "firsts" throughout this year. There will be the first Christmas without their loved one; the first birthday without them; the first time something breaks in the house; the first time they get sick; the first family event that must be attended alone; etc. Every time they experience one of these "firsts," it is as if their loved one dies all over again. They are hit with a strong wave of the feelings of grief and loss.

It is for this reason that, when we talk in chapter 10 of this book about the absolute necessity of "follow up," the primary emphasis will be on the first year. This is the time when the grieving will need their grief coach to be walking alongside them more than any other.

There are some specific events during that first year that are typically the most painful:

The First Weeks

The initial weeks following the death of a loved one are, to many, a blur. There is the planning for and then the attending of the viewing and funeral service and burial. Greeting all the people who come can be wonderful, yet also draining and painful. As difficult as that can be, it only gets worse. The friends and supporters then go home. Life gets back to normal rather quickly for everyone else. For the immediate family, however, the grieving has just started. In addition, for the survivors there is much additional work to be done. Affairs need to be settled quickly and efficiently. At the same time, grief is demanding attention, and the realization is beginning to set in that a deep and permanent change has just been thrust upon them. Those grieving are also beginning to realize that in addition to the primary loss of their loved one, many secondary losses (see chapter 4) are being experienced and are complicating the grief.

Because your grieving coachee is still in shock during these initial weeks, she is usually not ready to "go deep." One of the best things an end-of-life coach can do at this point is to make his presence and support known. Follow your coachee's lead as to when she is ready to go deeper. Follow her time frame. Often, assisting with practical matters is also helpful at this time.

Three Months

The three month time period is often difficult for those in grief. The grief and all the emotions that go with it seem to intensify. Those grieving usually have no clue why, but they surely experience it. Often what happens at this time period is that the shock and disbelief and denial are starting to wear off, and your coachee is beginning to face the reality of their loved one's death. Many of their friends and relatives have moved on, and instead of giving your coachee support, they are now pres-suring him to be freed from the pain of what has happened. When your coachee realizes he is not "over it," he feels shame, wondering what is wrong with him. This adds to the pain and complicates the grief.

The end-of-life coach can provide some needed support and care during this time period. Extra contacts are appreciated. The emotions are often extreme at this time, and having a coach to normalize their feelings and to provide a safe place to mourn is valued. Invite them to tell "their story," and attentively listen as they repeat it over and over and over again.

The Anniversary of the Death

Most people don't need a reminder of the first-year anniversary of their loved one's death. The intensity of grief comes rushing in with a pain that rivals the initial feelings of loss. The anticipation of the anniversary date can be as bad as, if not worse than, the anniversary itself.

Encouraging your coachees to talk through and to plan ahead as to how they want to spend the anniversary day can be a help to them. Contact and support on that day is usually appreciated. The anniversary might also be an opportunity for more healing to take place. Invitations for your coachee to honor himself, as he reflects on surviving the first year of grief, could create new awareness. There could possibly be ways your coachee can honor his loved one in some special way on that day, getting him involved in some action steps. It could be a day for him to tearfully tell the story of his loved one over again, as he honors the memories and the relationship he and his loved one shared. It is your coachee's day to spend as he desires. Your coaching presence, however, might be what he needs to help bring to the surface the opportunities for using this anniversary for him to move forward.

Holidays and Special Days

Holidays, birthdays, wedding anniversaries and other special days can be agonizing for those in grief. Facing these holidays can seem overwhelming. Holidays, more than any other days, can signify "family gatherings." At these times, your coachee will be acutely aware of the voids in his life. It is hard to be holly and jolly when the person you thought you'd spend your whole life with is gone. It is painful to find the perfect gift and to realize the person is no longer alive to receive it. All around your coachee, the sounds and sights and smells of the upcoming holiday will trigger memories of his loved one. For some, it is nearly impossible to smile and celebrate a special day when their heart is breaking. Because life as they knew it has changed, adjustments need to be made. It can be an opportunity to reassess the way special days are celebrated. Old traditions can be modified and new ones established. There is a lot your coachee might want to talk through in preparation for upcoming holidays and special days.

Articles and entire books are written on this subject. They can provide helpful insights and suggestions for surviving these days. The end-of-life coach will want to be aware of the difficulties of these days and offer his support and presence.

One awareness I want to remind you of is that, unlike the pretty scenes on the Christmas cards we send out, the first Christmas was messy and painful. Think of the confused teenaged mom who birthed her first child far from home, next to noisy animals in a smelly barn. Think of the Father who loves people so much that he gave His only Son over to poverty, pain, danger and death. Remember that not everyone was thrilled to learn of the coming of the long-awaited Messiah. Feeling threatened, Herod ordered a massacre of all baby boys under two years of age. If you listened carefully to the sounds of that first Christmas, you could hear soldier's threats, baby's cries, and young mothers wailing in desperation. Grief was present during that first Christmas.

6) Be the Student, Not the Expert

As stated in the section on coaching the dying, your attitude toward your coachee should be that of student. As we listen and learn, we will get to know our coachees in a deeper way. Through powerful questions, we can guide them into new awareness and deeper discovery about how to move forward in the journey of grief.

Approaching your coachee with the attitude of a student (rather than teacher) will encourage him to share more openly and deeply with you. He will know you are interested in what he has to say. It is this student attitude which will enable him to feel safe and heard, and to take charge of his own forward moving journey.

This student attitude will also cause the coach to listen more attentively. As a student, you don't come with your mind already made up. You don't enter a session with a lesson plan intact. You have to actively listen to determine what your coachee is really experiencing. Although there are aspects of grief that are similar across the board, the reality is that each grief experience is unique. Not only that, but what your coachee is experiencing one day might be completely different than what he is experiencing the next day. As a student you are always ready to learn and to meet your coachee wherever he is that day. You are eager to learn, because you know that the more you hear and understand, the better you can support your coachee and walk his journey with him. So your coachee will regularly hear you saying, "Teach me what it is like for you" and "Tell me more."

As a student, the coach is also willing to learn lessons that will apply to his own life. Note: the purpose is not for the coach to focus on his own needs. It is all about the coachee. If the coach has the attitude of a student, however, he will learn lessons that can impact his own life.

Some of my grieving coachees have taught me the importance of trusting God even when you are in the midst of some of the darkest times imaginable. Others regularly remind me of the importance of valuing the relationships I now have. Some teach me how to pour out my heart to God. Other coachees help me to understand more fully what love really means and provide for me living examples of what love in action looks like. Some teach me the importance of seeking and granting forgiveness, and the necessity of living with short accounts. I could go on. The learning never stops. I never want it to. So I continue to enter into my times with the grieving as a student. I enter with the anticipation and expectation that as long as I am willing to learn from my coachee, I will be a caring support to him along his journey. But I also come with the anticipation and expectation that my coachee has something to teach me by his life and example. My life is better because I have become a student of my coachees.

7) Help Them Discover Their New Normal

"Aren't you over it yet?" "Isn't it time you stop crying and get back to normal?"

Many equate grief with having a cold or the flu. You are sick for a time, but then you get over it and are back to normal again. Unfortunately, that is not the way grief works. A far better illustration of what grief is like is that of someone who has just had their leg amputated. The leg is permanently gone. It will never come back. Because of this amputation, this person's life from here on will be forever affected. With a lot of hard work, the amputee can hopefully live a full life again. He can get a prosthesis and learn anew how to walk. Yet, he will forever walk with a limp. He will never forget his "loss." His life will never be the same as it was before his amputation. He will never get back to "normal." Grief coaching empowers the amputee to create a new normal.

Coaching the grieving has to start with that safe place where the coachee can mourn. He needs to embrace his pain and all the emotions of grief. There is no time limit for this phase of the coaching. Each individual is different, and each coachee needs to be given the time that he needs. But coaching is always forward moving. It involves forming a new vision for the future. It involves brainstorming what that vision might look like as part of this new normal and what it will take for the coachee to get there. It includes the development of the strategies that will be used to get the coachee to where he wants to be, and identifies those individuals who will support and encourage, and be a companion to, the coachee along the way.

The seventh supporting building block reminds the end-of-life coach to keep this forward moving focus in mind while coaching the grieving. Your coachees will need support as they seek to discover their new normal.

Some of the areas where they might be searching for their new normal are:

A New Identity

The loss of a significant person means acquiring a new identity. Your coachee will never be quite the same as he was before his loved one died. That portion of his life is gone. When someone with whom one has a relationship dies, his self-identity, or the way he sees himself, naturally changes.

Listen to how people introduce themselves. "I am John's wife." "I am Mary's son." "I am Tim's daughter." "I am Johnny's father." When that other person by whom we describe ourselves dies, who are we then? That is something your coachee will need to figure out. He is in search of his new normal. Walking through this process with your coachee (and it is a process—often a long, slow, painful process) will be part of his forming a new vision for the future.

A New Relationship with the Person Who Died

The goal is not for your coachee to forget his loved one who died. Forming a new identity does not mean disregarding the old one. Rather, the goal is for your coachee to change his relationship with the departed from one of physical presence to that of memory. When a person dies, family and friends are flooded with memories of the deceased—memories of who the person was, things they had done together, funny times they had shared, sad or painful experiences, lessons that had been learned. So many memories flood the mind of the grieving. I regularly remind my coachees that these memories are precious gifts from God, which no one can take away from them. These memories are theirs to hold onto forever. Yet, I encourage them to not hold onto them. Rather, I invite them to share them with others. I encourage them to keep their loved one alive through the sharing of those memories.

Some powerful questions help develop this new relationship with the person who died: Tell me about your loved one. What made him special? What are the memories that are going through your mind? What would John do in this particular situation?

A New Group of Friends

Another aspect of your coachee searching for his new normal will include finding new friends with whom he will spend time. If your coachee's spouse has died, and the couple spent most of their time with other couples, chances are your coachee will not feel comfortable with this same group. A widow or widower can feel out of place with a group of married people.

Your coachee will also find that not everyone is supportive of him in his grief. Dr. Alan D. Wolfelt often talks about the rule of thirds (Wolfelt 2003, 127-8). One third of the people in your grieving coachee's life will be supportive friends. They will be "safe" people to share with and will encourage your coachee to do his work of mourning. Another third of the people in his life will turn out to be neutral in his response to grief. They will neither help nor hinder him in his journey. The final third of people in your coachee's life will be harmful in his effort to mourn well. They will judge him. They will try to get him to stop mourning, and they will not be interested in hearing his story.

Your coachee will need support as he seeks out people in the first group.

A New Sense of Purpose

When someone you love dies, it is normal to question your meaning and purpose in life. You may feel that when your loved one died, a part of you died with him. You wonder what reason there is to go on living.

Perhaps your coachee served as a caregiver for his wife. He got up every day and worked hard to serve her and care for her. He made a difference in her life and knew that she depended on him. He gladly gave his all to meet her needs. Now that she has died, however, what reason does he have to get out of bed? Is there any purpose for his life? Is there any meaning to his current existence?

Whatever your coachee's situation, his loss will cause him to search for a new normal. Included in that will be the discovery of a new sense of purpose.

A Renewed Relationship with God

"Why did my loved one die?" "How could God allow this to happen?" These are normal questions asked when a loved one dies. Some of those in grief draw close to God as a way of seeking help through their loss. Others experience times of doubt and question the very existence of God. Both responses are a means of seeking a new sense of meaning following their loss. This questioning is normal and is all part of searching for a new normal.

Once again, allow me to remind the end-of-life coach that it is not your job to lead your coachee to a new normal. The questions he will be asking are, for the most part, not questions you are to answer. The coach's role, through deep listening and powerful questions, is to walk with your coachee as he forms a new vision for his future. It will involve brainstorming what that vision might look like as part of his new normal. It will include the development of the strategies that will be used to get your coachee to where he wants to be, and it will entail identifying those individuals who will support, encourage and be a companion to your coachee along the way. Allow your coachee to go through the process. Encourage him to find within himself the answers to his questions. Support him as he continues to mourn as he works his way through. Discovering a new normal is not easy, but it is essential in moving forward in grief.

8) Celebrate Their Growth

Walking the journey of grief is life-changing. No one chooses to experience grief. It is almost always unwanted and unplanned. Yet for many, the journey of grief is a wonderfully growing experience.

One of the great privileges of an end-of-life coach is to be able to help your coachee realize his growth and to celebrate it with him.

Growth through grief comes in many forms. For some, it is an increased sensitivity toward people who are going through difficulties. For others, it is a better understanding of themselves. They are able to accomplish things they never dreamed possible, and move forward in life with increased confidence. Still others come through their grief journey with a commitment to give back what others have given them. They volunteer for hospice, or visit their church's shut-ins, or seek out those who are grieving a loss. Some learn to appreciate each moment of each day, learning what a gift life is. They live as fully as possible every single moment. Others realize growth in their relationship with God, get more involved in their church, and commit to serving or sharing their faith more diligently. The list is endless…

Affirm your grieving coachee when he begins to recognize some of this growth. Watch to see how he is living out what he has learned. Encourage him to go deeper by asking questions like, "What have you learned from this loss?" or "How has this grief made you a better person?" or "What has this journey of grief taught you that you couldn't have learned any other way?"

Some days will be difficult and painful. The grieving will need regular times of affirmation and support (see chapter 10). But don't forget to celebrate their growth along the way.

Chapter Nine

Children

This book would be incomplete if I did not mention a few words about children. I wish it would not be necessary—but it is. Some children die. Most children experience the death of someone they love. All children grieve.

As an end-of-life coach, it is likely that you will have opportunities to coach children in end-of-life issues. It is almost a certainty that you will coach adults about the place of children in end-of-life issues. The questions are raised constantly. Should children take part in funerals or other post-death rituals? Is it permissible for a child to see a dead body? Should I talk to my child about death? Do children grieve? Is it not my role as a parent to protect my child from having to deal with end-of-life issues?

As an end-of-life coach, these are questions I deal with on a regular basis. However, more often than not, these issues are not posed as questions, but rather as facts or even as commands. My child will not be permitted to attend the funeral! It's not right! I will not cry or grieve in the presence of my child! It is not healthy for her to see that! I will protect my child from dealing with end-of-life issues, just like my parents did for me! (Interestingly, those who issue these commands were usually raised by parents who believed the same way.)

As adults, these people are often terrified about end-of-life issues. They are the ones who will not go into the room of their loved one who has died. They will not talk openly about death. They are uncomfortable attending funerals. Their parents' sincere attempts to "protect them" only caused them to be ill-equipped to deal with one of the most basic realities of life. And now they want to give that same "protection" to their own children.

The truth of the matter is, the best way to protect a child is not to pretend that death doesn't happen and that grief isn't real. The best way to protect a child is to give them the keys to know how to face the reality of death, and to mourn all the inevitable losses that are part of life on this earth.

Children do not naturally fear death. Think about it. Fear is something that we as parents and we as a society instill in them. We put a black shroud around it and worry it into power. There is no mistreatment in allowing children to learn that their loved ones, their pets, and eventually they will die. On the contrary, it is a gift of love.

The Keys to Coaching Children in End of Life Issues

In order to coach children in end-of-life issues, or to coach adults about the place of children in end-of-life issues, we must be aware of some of the basics.

Remember the Building Blocks

All the building blocks described previously are applicable to the coaching of and about children. That is the place to start.

When to Talk About It

After the law was given to the people of Israel, we read these words in Deuter-onomy 6:6-9:

> These commandments that I give you today are to be on your hearts. Impress them on your children. Talk about them when you sit at home and when you walk along the road, when you lie down and when you get up. Tie them as symbols on your hands and bind them on your foreheads. Write them on the doorframes of your houses and on your gates.

We should teach our children about death using the same method. When we see leaves change color on a tree and eventually fall to the ground, when we come across a dead bird in the yard, when we watch the movie "Bambi" or another show where someone or something dies, when a pet is hit by a car, or a goldfish is found floating in the fish tank – these are all opportunities to teach that death is a natural and normal part of life on this earth.

When the death of a family member or other loved one occurs, the opportunity for teaching only increases. Children must learn that when it comes to people, as the writer of Ecclesiastes said, "There is a time to be born and a time to die." This is also a wonderful opportunity to talk about heaven, or whatever one's views of the afterlife might be.

Children's Concepts of Death and Grief

Before talking to children about death and grief, it is important to understand that different ages view death and experience grief differently. At each age, our ideas and our beliefs—in other words, our concepts—change.

For further exploration, there are whole books written on this topic. For our purposes, please review the table below, reprinted by permission from The New England Journal of Medicine (2004, 350:17).

Age Range	Characteristics	Predominant Concepts of Death	Spiritual Development	Interventions
0–2 yr	Has sensory and motor relationship with environment Has limited language skills Achieves object permanence May sense that something is wrong	None	Faith reflects trust and hope in others Need for sense of self-worth and love	Provide maximal physical comfort, familiar persons and transitional objects (favorite toys), and consistency Use simple physical communication
>2–6 yr	Uses magical and animistic thinking Is egocentric Thinking is irreversible Engages in symbolic play Developing language skills	Believes death is temporary and reversible, like sleep Does not personalize death Believes death can be caused by thoughts	Faith is magical and imaginative Participation in ritual becomes important Need for courage	Minimize separation from parents Correct perceptions of illness as punishment Evaluate for sense of guilt and assuage if present Use precise language (dying, dead)
>6–12 yr	Has concrete thoughts	Development of adult concepts of death Understands that death can be personal Interested in physiology and details of death	Faith concerns right and wrong May accept external interpretations as the truth Connects ritual with personal identity	Evaluate child's fears of abandonment Be truthful Provide concrete details if requested Support child's efforts to achieve control and mastery Maintain access to peers Allow child to participate in decision making
>12–18 yr	Generality of thinking Reality becomes objective Capable of self-reflection Body image and self-esteem paramount	Explores nonphysical explanations of death	Begins to accept internal interpretations as the truth Evolution of relationship with God or higher power Searches for meaning, purpose, hope, and value of life	Reinforce child's self-esteem Allow child to express strong feelings Allow child privacy Promote child's independence Promote access to peers Be truthful Allow child to participate in decision making

Table 3. Development of Death Concepts and Spirituality in Children.

Listen

The place to start is always listening, not speaking. This is true in coaching children as well as adults. Adults should never assume they know exactly how children feel when they are dealing with an end-of-life issue. Children can teach adults what the experience is uniquely like for them. The end-of-life coach should provide a safe, caring place, where children can share freely and openly.

Be Honest

In speaking to a child about dying, death and grief, the next key is to always be honest. If you don't tell your children the truth, what they imagine will usually be worse. In addition, children can tell if you are not telling them the truth. To say that Grandmother has gone on a long trip and will no longer be here is a lie. The family member or well-meaning friend who tries to keep the truth from children is usually not the one who has to explain later why they were not respected enough or trusted enough to be told the truth. When the truth is discovered, the child is likely to feel betrayed, left out, and deeply hurt.

Use Real Words

As a way to "protect" children, instead of telling them that a loved one has died, many will say things like, "Grandmother has gone to sleep," or "We lost her," or "She passed away," or "She has gone to a better place." These words can be deceptive to a child. Often we don't think about the powerful implications of our euphemisms:

- If we tell children that Grandmother has gone on a really long trip, they may believe that Grandmother has abandoned them.

- If we tell them that Grandmother has gone to sleep, they may become afraid to go to bed or may start having nightmares.

- If we tell them we lost Grandmother, they may want to start an all out search for her.

- If we tell them that God has taken Grandmother away, they may believe that a cruel God snatches good people away.

- If we tell them that Grandmother was so good that God wanted her to be with Him, they may fear being good.

- If we tell them that death is darkness and nothingness, they may become afraid of the dark.

Part of being honest and speaking the truth is using real, simple, clear, direct words to describe what has occurred.

Help Them Express Their Feelings

Children need confirmation from adults that it's all right to be sad and to cry, and that the hurt they feel now won't last forever. They need to know that their feelings are appropriate. Children have to learn how to grieve, just as they learn how to ride a bicycle or play the piano. The adults in their lives are their models. They will learn to grieve and to express their feelings by watching you. That is why it is important for adults to allow the children in their lives to see them mourn. It may be upsetting to see Mommy or Daddy cry, but it's even more upsetting to be pushed out of the room when they know that Daddy is about to burst into tears.

As children express their feelings, adults need to respond with sensitivity and warmth. Be aware of tone of voice. Be sure to maintain eye contact. What is communicated without words can be just as meaningful to children as what is actually said. Let children know their feelings will be accepted and that they will not be judged or criticized during this painful time.

Provide Memories and Keepsakes

As in coaching adults, children will be greatly helped when given the opportunity to share their memories, and to hold on to some physical objects that will remind them of their loved one.

Use Available Resources

There are many, age appropriate resources available that can aid in coaching children in end-of-life issues. They include books, videos, journals, coloring books, games, etc. The end-of-life coach will do well to make himself familiar with these resources.

Funerals and Other Post-Death Rituals

Since many of your coachees will likely ask you about the involvement of their children in funerals and other end-of-life rituals, allow me to share a few of my thoughts on the matter:

- Children should have the same opportunity to preview the body and/or attend the service as any other member of the family. Attendance increases the opportunity for open and honest sharing about what has occurred, and provides great opportunity for teaching about end-of-life issues.

- Although encouraged, children should never be forced to attend.

- If parents will be busy at the ceremony and cannot attend to their children, they should be placed in the care of another trusted adult.

- Allowing children to help plan the funeral can be rewarding. Although they might not completely understand all the details of this ceremony, their involvement can help establish a sense of comfort. It can also help in the affirmation that life goes on, even though their loved one has died.

- Children need to know ahead of time what they will see and experience at the funeral. They should be told what will happen, who will be there, where they will be sitting, how long it will last, the flowers that may be present, and that people will probably be expressing a wide variety of emotions. They need to be reminded that it is natural for people to cry.

- Children should have someone with them at all times to provide comfort and support.

- Follow-up after the funeral is crucial. Talk about what has happened, what it meant, and what they thought about it. Help them express their emotions. Adults need to be good observers of children's behavior at the funeral. Unknowingly, children will be showing what the death means to them.

- Parents, just like the end-of-life coach, must explore their own personal feelings about death. (See chapter 11.) Until they consciously examine their own concerns, doubts and fears about death, it will be difficult to support children when a loved one has died.

Chapter Ten

Follow Up. Follow Up. Follow Up.

Spiritual leaders, please read carefully. This chapter might be, for you, the most important chapter in this whole book. "Follow Up" is repeated three times in the title of this chapter for emphasis. It is that important.

In my work as a Hospice Chaplain and Bereavement Coordinator, I interact with people from many different beliefs, denominations and spiritual groups. The sad comment I hear all too often by those dealing with an end-of-life issue is, "My church/spiritual group/ spiritual leader does not support me very well." As these individuals keep talking, the oft-repeated issue emerges—a lack of follow up.

Having spent 15 years in pastoral ministry, I completely understand the other side of this issue. Clergy do not have the time or the resources (and often the knowledge) to keep track of all the needed information and to provide the follow up desired. This chapter will help to make follow up care manageable and effective.

Follow Up of the Dying

Be Available

Making an initial visit and coaching the dying, as described in chapter 7, will be meaningful to both the dying and his family. What is needed by all involved, however, is the knowledge that their spiritual support will continue to be available as needed. The assurance that you are there for them throughout this whole journey will be one of the greatest gifts you can give the dying and his family. (And at the same time, to many, that will become the needed reminder that God is there for them.)

For the dying, that does not necessarily mean being with them 24/7. The dying need time alone. The dying need time alone with their families. Spiritual leaders' visits with the dying will sometimes last an hour, but sometimes only 10 or 15 minutes. Overstaying your welcome will negate your ministry to them. As long as you continue to stay available and follow their lead as to how often you should visit/coach them, you will do well. Remember, it is all about them. I will usually ask the dying and/or the families outright what their desires are, and how I can best support them along this journey. If I am visiting and, after 10 minutes, notice the dying is getting sleepy, I will ask if it would be helpful for me to pray for them and then leave so they can get some sleep. I will say, "I am here as a support to you. I realize that sometimes the best way I can help is by leaving." This is appreciated and, when I do this, the patient and family are quick to invite me back. Those who overstay their welcome are often not invited back and lose their opportunity for continued ministry. Regular text messages or voice mails stating that you are thinking about them and praying for them can help as well. The journey toward death can be a lonely journey. Knowing their spiritual leader is available for them and with them will be a great support for certain.

Hospice Care

Sometimes the dying and their families are not aware of a helpful support system that is available to them. It is covered by Medicare and most insurance companies. End-of-life coaches will do well to be aware of hospice and what hospice care entails, so a referral, if needed, can be made to your dying coachee. Your local hospice will be happy to give you detailed information about their hospice program. Allow me to explain a few of the basics here.

Hospice is a philosophy of care that gives holistic support to a person with a terminal condition. To be eligible for hospice, an individual has to have been given a six months or less prognosis from their doctor. Physical, emotional and spiritual support is given to both the dying and their families. Dame Cicely Saunders, the founder of hospice, said, "You matter to the last moment of your life, and we will do all we can, not only to help you die peacefully, but to live until you die."

The philosophy of hospice is that "Hospice affirms life and neither hastens nor postpones death. Coordinated interdisciplinary holistic care enables the patient to remain at home with the support of caregivers."

The best way I know how to explain hospice is by means of a parable, written by the hospice nurse, Lois Kinsella, RN, BSN, MS. It is entitled, "Walking the Hundred-Mile Road" (Kinsella 2001).

> *I've been traveling the hundred-mile road for many years. As I set out one beautiful spring day, the birds were singing sweetly. Next to the road, early flowers were popping out in splendid colors.*

Rounding a bend, I came upon a man going in the same direction carrying a red and a black sack on his back. They seemed quite heavy, but he didn't complain. We struck up a conversation.

I introduced myself as the "companion who walks the hundred-mile road and helps carry and unload sacks." He told me his name was Bert.

I asked if I could help him carry or unload the sacks. He said no; he'd rather carry them himself. He did say that "maybe down the road" he'd let me help.

Bidding him farewell, I continued on my way. Pretty soon, I came upon a young woman carrying black, red, and yellow sacks. They looked similar to Bert's, so I asked where she got them. She replied that every now and then she'd find a sack with her name on it by the roadside. She assumed she was supposed to pick it up and carry it.

I couldn't help but feel compassion for this woman; she was so young and so heavily laden. I asked if I could help her carry her load or empty the sacks. She appreciated the offer but seemed reluctant to accept. Struggling with my offer, she said that "maybe down the road" she'd need help.

Again I went on my way, not wanting to force myself on anyone. But I felt confused. Why was my sincere offer to help being turned down repeatedly?

Close to the end of the hundred-mile road, I came across an old man and his wife. They looked so tired. He was carrying several sacks: a black one, a small red one, a yellow one, a large bright orange sack, and a green one. His wife tried her best to help him, but she was too frail to bear the weight. I introduced myself and asked if I could help.

Without hesitation, they replied, "Oh yes, yes! We can hardly put one foot in front of the other and we need to get to the end of the hundred-mile road. We're so close, but we don't think we can make it."

I took the sacks off the old man's back and simply laid them by the roadside. We all walked along together, talking about the hundred-mile road and how difficult the journey had been.

Relieved of their burdens, the man and woman went to the edge of the road and began to smell the wildflowers. He picked a handful and gave them to her and told her how much he loved her.

As we approached the end of the hundred-mile road, it became clear that the old man was going to cross alone onto the endless road, and his wife would go back. Needless to say, their parting was emotional, but it overflowed with good feelings. They said to me, "Once you came along and helped with our sacks and gave us time to enjoy each other a little longer, it just seemed easier to say good-bye."

The old man left after his wife told him it was okay to go. She cried. I asked her to return with me. On the way, we met the young woman. Now carrying a black sack, a very large red one, and orange, yellow, green, and purple ones, she looked tired but still refused help. Again she said, "Maybe down the road."

Disappointed, the wife and I continued our journey home. As you might expect, we met Bert still struggling with his load. The old man's wife tried to convince Bert to let someone help with his sacks, but Bert just said, "Maybe down the road" and went on his way.

The old man's wife and I continued to her home. I told her I'd stop by from time to time to check on her. We could have tea or walk in her garden or just sit together. She again thanked me for helping.

After a rest, I started on the hundred-mile road again. Very near the end, I came across Bert and the young woman, both exhausted. They sat at the edge of the road, hardly able to speak, with their sacks piled on and around them. Crossing over to the endless road was very difficult.

I started to remove and unload the sacks: the black sack filled with sadness and despair, the red one with anger, the yellow one with anxiety, the orange sack with physical pain, the green one with fear, and the purple sack filled with spiritual questions.

Bert and the young woman, their eyes filled with tears, looked up and said, "Thank you. We're so sorry we didn't see way back down the road what you could do for us. Please tell others our story so no one will have to walk the hundred-mile road alone."

With that, they both got up and crossed over for their journey on the endless road.

Hospice helps people with terminal conditions to carry and to unload their sacks, so that their journey to the end of life will be as peaceful as possible.

Just as is the case with grieving (see chapter 5), there are a number of myths concerning hospice. Allow me to briefly share with you some of the common ones.

Myth #1 – Hospice Is a Place.

Hospice is a philosophy of care, not necessarily a specific place. There are some inpatient hospice facilities, but hospice takes place wherever the need exists. About 80% of hospice care takes place in the person's home. Other places include nursing homes, assisted living facilities or hospitals.

Myth #2 – Hospice Hastens Death.

Hospice in no way hastens a person's death. Some people actually live longer and more comfortably because of the extra care they receive while on hospice. On the other hand, hospice doesn't prolong death either. Hospice allows the death process to proceed at a normal and natural pace. Hospice views death as a natural occurrence and has the goal of allowing people to die with dignity and with their symptoms under control.

Myth #3 – Hospice Is Only for People with Cancer.

Hospice is available for patients with any life-limiting illness in which the physician has determined that the patient's life expectancy is six months or less, and that comfort measures, rather than curative measures, are not appropriate or chosen by the patient.

This could include illnesses such as congestive heart failure, emphysema, AIDS, ALS and advanced Alzheimer's disease.

Myth #4 – Hospice is Only for Old People.

Although the majority of hospice patients are older, hospices serve patients of all ages, including children.

Myth #5 – Hospice Care Is for Those in Their Final Days.

This myth describes the thought that one comes onto hospice only when they are just days or hours away from dying (what we call deathbed intervention). For some this is true, but it is far better when the dying come onto hospice much earlier, giving the hospice team a good amount of time to get to know the dying, minister to them, and help them to work through the end-of-life issues.

Myth #6 – You Must be Ready to Die to be Ready for Hospice.

This is not true. One of the goals of hospice is to help the patient deal with the fact that they are dying and to help them prepare for it. That's why there is a whole team of people to help.

Myth #7 − Hospice Is Only for Dying People.

As stated earlier, the focus is not only on the dying patient, but also on the family or caregivers.

Myth #8 − Hospice Provides 24-Hour Care.

Hospice provides intermittent visits, but not 24-hour, seven-day a week care. The other requirement for coming onto hospice is that there must be a caregiver present. This could be a family member, a paid caregiver, or a hospital or other facility.

Myth #9 − Hospice Care Is Expensive.

Many are entitled to the Medicare Hospice Benefit, which covers virtually all hospice services and requires little, if any, out of pocket costs. The fact is, hospice is a major way for many people to save money. There are no financial burdens incurred by the family, in sharp contrast to the huge financial expenses at the end of life which are incurred when hospice is not used.

Myth #10 − You Must be Homebound to Receive Hospice Care.

There are no activity limitations for patients enrolled in the hospice program. Patients are encouraged to enjoy all aspects of life as fully as possible.

Myth #11 − Once You Sign Onto Hospice, There's No Getting Out of It.

A person can sign off hospice any time they would like. Some choose to do this to go back to aggressive treatment. Also, if a patient's condition improves, as sometimes happens, they can even be dropped from hospice care for a time. And if the patient lives longer than six months, but continues to show decline, they can stay on hospice.

Myth #12 − Hospice Care Means Giving Up Hope and Waiting Passively to Die.

Some do just this, but the goal of hospice is for the opposite to happen. It is for the patient and family to live as fully as possible until the end. For some, the last months/weeks of life can be the best they ever had. Hospice is all about hope – the hope just has a changing focus.

Myth #13 − Death is the Worst Thing that Can Happen.

Death will come to all of us. Death is, after all, just another natural stage in the life of a human being. There are many things worse than death, such as: alienation from those we love, persistent pain, worry about the well-being of the ones we must leave behind, and loneliness that occurs from the abandonment by friends and family who can't handle our approaching deaths. Hospice works hard to overcome all of these.

Follow Up of the Grieving

I went to visit a man whose wife had just died on our hospice services. He was a gruff man. He wore a patch over one eye and reminded me in both appearance and personality of a pirate. After our initial greetings, this man asked me why I was there. I explained my desire to support him along his journey of grief. He quickly informed me that he had no grief. "Dead is dead," this man said. "I must move on. So you may leave." I assure you that is far more the exception than the rule. Most of those who are grieving long for continued support and follow up. Even if they don't sit down to be coached by you, they want to know someone remembers. They want to know someone cares. They want to know someone is there for them if they need them. They want to know that their spiritual leader (and their God) is available.

First Year Care

As stated in chapter 8, "Coaching The Grieving," the most intensive time for follow up and support is in the first year following the death. Your coachee will be working through all the emotions of grief, as well as experiencing all the "firsts." If you are privileged to be able to set up regular visits/coaching sessions with your grieving coachee, you will do well to follow their lead as far as desired frequency. Initial contact should be made following the death. Contact at the three-month point will be helpful. Ongoing teaching on the journey of grief and the necessity to mourn will be invaluable. The availability of helpful classes or grief support groups should be communicated with your grieving coachees. Contact at the time of their deceased loved one's birthday and on the anniversary of their death will show great care and concern. Special TLC should be given during the holidays, when their pain will most likely be intensified. Periodic phone calls to say that you care and that you are available will mean the world to your grieving coachees.

How are you feeling having read the above paragraph? If you are feeling overwhelmed, and thinking that giving that amount of first year follow up to all your grieving parishioners is impossible, you are in the norm. This is the reason why follow up is often not done, and why many of the grieving feel alone and unsupported.

There is a clear disconnect between what critically needs to be done and what is virtually impossible for most pastors to do (unless they have a large staff who can manage this for them). As a result, a software program has been developed just for you. It is called the "Bereavement Management System (BMS)." It has been created by the Bereavement Management Group (of which I am a part). Information about purchasing this software can be found at www.bereavementmanagement.com. The program allows you to create personalized cards (including the deceased's name and family members' name), letters and newsletters. The cards are automatically created and ready to be sent out at the time of death, on the deceased's birthday, at the holidays, and at the anniversary of the death. Letters are created immediately following the death, and again after the first year of care. Twelve editions of your grief newsletter are created monthly. Monthly phone lists are created showing which grieving individuals are at one month, three months, six months and nine months along their grief journey. The necessary information to call each family member is also present, making the phone calls as easy as possible. In addition, other useful tools are included to support your grieving coachees and to manage your spiritual group's grief support program.

Whether or not BMS is used, your grieving coachees are longing for follow up and support along their grief journey.

Long Term Care

Even though the first year is the most intensive, follow up needs to continue beyond the first year. For this reason, the Long Term Edition of BMS provides ongoing yearly birthday, holiday and anniversary cards, phone call reminders, additional letters, newsletters, and spontaneous cards that can be designed and created when needed.

Regardless of the method you choose for follow up, know that your continual care will mean more to them than words can express. Your support will also make you look like the most caring spiritual leader there is!

Group Coaching

Some grieving individuals find comfort in being with others who understand what they are going through. This is the purpose of grief support groups. These groups are safe places where grieving people can share their story and can receive grief instruction, as well as caring support. The end-of-life coach will want to be aware of the grief support groups in his area, so that if desired by his coachee, a referral can be made.

The end-of-life coach might want to begin his own group within his spiritual community. Here group coaching principles should be used to support and care for those in grief. A helpful resource is a Christian-based DVD series created for use in grief support groups, entitled *Grief Share*. Information for purchasing this series can be found at www.griefshare. org.

Follow Up. Follow Up. Follow Up. Whatever means you choose to use, your dying and grieving coachees are in need of regular, ongoing follow up. Let them know you haven't forgotten them. Let them know you care.

> *Religion that God our Father accepts as pure and faultless is this: to look after orphans and widows in their distress and to keep oneself from being polluted by the world.*
> —*James 1:27*

Chapter Eleven

The End-of-Life Coach

Y ou have started reading the eleventh and final chapter of this book, *Coaching at End of Life*. Although this is the end of the book, it is probably the first place where an end-of-life coach should start reading. Until we personally work through the material in this chapter, we should not attempt to do anything else that is written in this book. Before we can effectively coach someone who is dying, we must work through our own issues concerning dying. Likewise, before we can effectively coach someone who is in the midst of grief, we must work through our own issues of grief and loss. Finally, before we coach anyone at end of life, it is imperative that we think through the self-care principles listed in this chapter. Coaching people at end of life can be draining. If precautions are not taken, burnout is a very real possibility. The purpose of this final chapter is to aid the end-of-life coach in starting his ministry as a healthy coach, and to enable him to emerge from his time with the dying and the grieving just as healthy, or hopefully even healthier.

We Are a Mist

I received a prayer request today for a friend of mine. My friend is a chaplain and is a part of the same denomination in which I serve. My friend has served as the chaplain in a large hospital. He has ministered to countless numbers of people who have been patients there. The prayer request stated that my friend was now himself a patient at that hospital. He was on a breathing tube and was struggling to stay alive, having just come through cancer surgery.

Reading that, I couldn't help but reflect on the reality of the brevity of life. James 4:14 says, "We are a mist that appears for a little while and then vanishes." The time will come when you will die. How does that make you feel? What emotions does it bring to the surface? What fears do you have? Do you have any regrets? Are you concerned about the process of death? How about your relationships—are there things that need to be done or said before you die? How is your bucket list coming? What will happen to you after you die? Is your eternal destiny secure?

These are the questions that will be brought to the mind of the end-of-life coach over and over again. Every time you sit down with someone who is dying and listen to his story, you will be reminded that you are a mist. This is normal. You won't change that. This can be helpful, as it gives you the continual opportunity to reassess your priorities and to make sure that you are living fully every day.

The time to work through those questions, however, is now—not when you are sitting with your coachee. Your coaching session is all about him. Your focus must be on him and his story. If you are responding to your own feelings that you are a mist, you will not be able to actively listen and respond to your coachee as you must.

Reflect on the questions in the exercises that follow. Then find a friend or fellow coach (preferably another end-of-life coach) with whom you can talk these things through.

Where Am I?

We are a mist that appears for a little while and then vanishes. —James 4:14

Fact: The time will come when you will die.

- How does that make you feel?

- What emotions does it bring to the surface?

- What fears do you have?

- Do you have any regrets?

- Are you concerned about the process of death?

- How about your relationships—are there things that need to be done or said before you die?

- How is your bucket list coming?

- What will happen to you after you die?

- Is your eternal destiny secure?

- Imagine that you just received news that you are dying. What is your reaction?

What Is Most Important

The following exercise will help you understand something about your dying patients. For the full effect of this exercise, complete each instruction before reading ahead.

Write down three things that are most important to you in your life

1.

2.

3.

Now look at your list. You have to give one of them up. Which one will you give up? Put a line through one of them.

You now have to give up one more. Cross it out.

What do you have left?

I have given this exercise to hundreds of people from all walks of life. Ninety-nine percent of the time I hear two things that people are left with. When I am speaking to secular groups, the one thing that is almost always left—the thing that is MOST IMPORTANT—is family. Over 99% of the time that is the answer left on people's papers. When I speak to religious groups, the thing left is usually their relationship with God, with family coming in a close second.

What were you left with as being most important?

When it comes to people who are approaching end of life, they will focus their attention on that which is most important. Usually what is desired is time spent with their families.

A 1992 nationwide Gallup Poll revealed that, given six months to live, 9 out of 10 Americans (87%) said that their choice at end of life would be to be cared for and to die in their own home or a family member's home, rather than in the hospital or somewhere else. They would prefer to be surrounded by their family and spend their last moments with them. My guess is that given that poll today, the number would be even higher.

I suggest that the end-of-life coach work through this exercise, and come to grips with what is most important to him, so that he can better understand and minister to his coachees.

How Do You Want to Die?

When you think about dying, what would you like your death to be like? Answer the following questions:

How would you like to die?

Where do you want to be?

Who should be there with you?

Do you want heroic measures taken to keep you alive?

What would you like to be wearing? A suit or dress? Sweat pants? A nightgown?

What music should be playing?

Look carefully at what you have written. These death scenes you've planned for yourself are what you will soon be projecting on your coachees. If you want to die with soft music playing and incense in the air, that's your choice. But be careful not to insist that your coachees do the same. If they want to die in peace or in chaos, with rock music or soft music, that's their choice. To force your beliefs or desires on them is to rob them of their dignity.

Dying with dignity means knowing that your death will be just as meaningful and purposeful as your life has been. It means dying the way you want to die, not the way others have deemed proper or worthy for you. Dying with dignity means being you, just as you have always been, right up to the end.

The end-of-life coach will do well to be aware of his own desires before he begins coaching, so as not to force his personal desires onto his coachees.

Dealing with Past Losses

Understanding your own personal losses and the grief you experienced is essential for end-of-life coaches. Earlier I stated that in order to live well and love well, one must mourn well. All the losses that we have experienced through life must be mourned. If we don't mourn those losses and, instead, stuff our grief emotions deep down inside, our lives will be affected. That grief will be looking for a way out, and usually not in a positive manner. In addition, every time you meet with a grieving coachee, your grief will be stirred within you. Stirring that grief and forcing you to deal with it is a positive thing. But dealing with it while you are coaching another is not good. Now is the time to deal with those losses.

Look at the questions below, as a way of conducting your own loss inventory. Review them yourself, or talk them through with a coach (preferably another end-of-life coach). Allow these questions to help you reflect on how your past losses are influencing your life today:

1. Reflect on one of the earliest significant losses in your life.

    - When did it happen?

    - How old were you?

    - Where was it?

    - Who were the people involved?

    - What actually happened?

    Below is a list of common losses to spur on your thinking:

• moving	• divorce	• illness
• loss of special possession	• end of relationship	• changing schools
• rejection	• downsizing	• loss of pets
• empty nest	• fire or theft	• loss of reputation
• job related	• innocence	• dreams/hopes

- incarceration of loved one • death of a loved one • health problems

- developmental transitions • abandonment/betrayal

2. What were your feelings at the time?

3. What were your reactions to the loss?

4. Did anyone give you suggestions or advice on how to handle the loss?

5. What did you learn about loss as a result of your early experience? Can you remember any statements that have stayed with you through the years?

6. What did you learn then that may be hindering the way you cope with loss today?

7. What did you learn about loss at an early age that helps you today?

Think specifically now, about your first experience of the death of a loved one, and how you grieved:

1. Who was it who died?

2. How old were you?

3. How did you learn about this first death?

4. What were you told?

5. Were you protected or included?

6. What will you teach your children that is the same and what will be different?

Reflect on your first viewing of a body:

1. Were you made to look at the body or told not to peek?

2. Were you told what you would see?

3. Did you hear ghost stories about bodies suddenly sitting up in the casket? Of people being buried alive? Of children being forced to kiss the corpse?

What were your family superstitions?

1. Does your family have any rituals, customs or superstitions related to death, funerals or burial?

2. Did anyone ever say to you, "Don't do that! Something bad will happen to you"?

3. What old messages hang on around the mystery of death? How do you feel when you think of them?

How did you show your feelings?

1. Were you allowed to cry?

2. Were you scolded or reprimanded for your feelings?

3. Were you told "not to be _____"? (Fill in your own blank).

4. Were you left to fend for yourself and find answers wherever you could?

Now think of the most recent loss you have experienced:

1. Identify the specific loss. Where? What? Who? When?

   - Spouse
   - Mother
   - Father
   - Sister
   - Brother
   - Grandmother
   - Grandfather
   - Aunt
   - Uncle
   - Cousin
   - Friend
   - Pet
   - Other

2. What were your feelings at the time?

3. What were your reactions to the loss?

4. Do you ever talk about the person who died? How often?

5. Did anyone give you suggestions or advice on how to handle the loss?

6. Did a friend or family member help you during/after the death?

   If yes, how did they help?

   - Talk about the death
   - Looking at pictures
   - Spending time with me
   - Pray with me
   - Give me hugs
   - Keep me safe
   - Answer my questions
   - Share feelings with me
   - Other
   - Talking about the person who died

7. What did you learn about loss as a result of your experience? How did others suggest you handle it?

8. How did your early experiences with loss affect the way you responded to this loss?

9. When you think about this loss now, are there any things you wish had been different?

10. List three healthy things you will do to respond to the next loss you encounter?

Now that you have reflected on those losses, look at the following statements and check the box that most applies to how you feel.

	Rarely/ Never	Sometimes	Often	All The Time
1. I have difficulties with trust and intimacy.				
2. I am anxious and have panic attacks.				
3. I do not feel like eating.				
4. I feel like hitting someone.				
5. I feel like hurting myself.				
6. I have a negative outlook on life.				
7. I struggle with substance abuse, addictions or eating disorders				
8. I find it difficult to express my feelings.				
9. I feel lonely.				
10. I find it easier to take care of others than to care for myself.				
11. I find it difficult to ask for what I want from others.				

Answering "often" or "all the time" to any of these statements can be a sign that there is loss in your life that has not been dealt with. Again, talk this through with your end-of-life coach.

Self-Care for the End-of-Life Coach

When you care for those who are dying and grieving, it is critical to find ways to care for yourself as well. The work of an end-of-life coach is draining—physically, emotionally and spiritually. As a result we must practice daily, ongoing, nurturing self-care in each of those three areas.

Physically, it is important to practice proper nutrition, get enough rest and exercise regularly. Emotionally, the end-of-life coach must find ways to nurture himself, reduce tension and stress, and connect with others with whom feelings, worries and thoughts can be expressed. Spiritually, time must be taken for renewal – whether through prayer and meditation, nature, or by whatever means we best renew our spirits.

Self-care is important for ourselves and our families. We will not be able to live fully if we do not take seriously the toll that being involved in this ministry can bring. But self-care is also important for the sake of our coachees. We owe it to them to be our best. Poor self-care will keep us from being fully present with them.

A resource that I recommend for each end-of-life coach is Dr. Alan D. Wolfelt's book, *Companioning You: A Soulful Guide to Caring for Yourself While You Care for the Dying and the Bereaved* (2012).

Dr. Wolfelt includes in this book what he calls "A Self-Care Manifesto for Caregivers to the Dying and the Bereaved" (Wolfelt, 2012). I will conclude this book with his important reminder to all who are privileged to serve as end-of-life coaches.

We who care for the bereaved and the dying have a wondrous opportunity: to help others embrace and grow through grief and to lead fuller, more deeply-lived lives ourselves because of this important work.

But our work is draining—physically, emotionally and spiritually. We must first care for ourselves if we want to care well for others. This manifesto is intended to empower you to practice good self-care.

1. I deserve to lead a joyful, whole life.
No matter how much I love and value my work, my life is multi-faceted. My family, my friends, my other interests and my spirituality also deserve my time and attention. I deserve my time and attention.

2. My work does not define me.
I am a unique, worthy person outside my work life. While relationships can help me feel good about myself, they are not what is inside me. Sometimes I need to stop "doing" and instead focus on simply "being."

3. I am not the only one who can help dying and bereaved people.

When I feel indispensable, I tend to ignore my own needs. There are many talented caregivers in my community who can also help the dying and the bereaved.

4. I must develop healthy eating, sleeping and exercise patterns.

I am aware of the importance of these things for those I help, but I may neglect them myself. A well-balanced diet, adequate sleep and regular exercise allow me to be the best I can be.

5. I may have forgotten how to take care of myself.

I may need to rediscover ways of caring for and nurturing myself. I may need to relearn how to explore my own feelings instead of focusing on everybody else's.

6. I must maintain boundaries in my helping relationships.

As a death caregiver, I cannot avoid getting emotionally involved with dying and bereaved people. Nor would I want to. Active empathy allows me to be a good companion to them. However, I must remember I am responsible to others, not for others.

7. I am not perfect and I must not expect myself to be.

I often wish my helping efforts were always successful. But even when I offer compassionate, "on-target" help, the recipient of that help isn't always prepared to use it. And when I do make mistakes, I should see them as an integral part of learning and growth, not as measurements of my self-worth.

8. I must practice effective time-management skills.

I must set practical goals for how I spend my time. I must also remember Pareto's principle: twenty percent of what I do nets eighty percent of my results.

9. I must also practice setting limits and alleviating stresses I can do something about.

I must work to achieve a clear sense of expectations and set realistic deadlines. I should enjoy what I do accomplish in helping others, but shouldn't berate myself for what is beyond me.

10. I must listen to my inner voice.

As a caregiver to the dying and the bereaved, I will at times become grief overloaded. When my inner voice begins to whisper its fatigue, I must listen carefully and allow myself some grief down-time.

11. I should express the personal me in both my work and play.

I shouldn't be afraid to demonstrate my unique talents and abilities. I must also make time each day to remind myself of what is important to me. If I only had three months to live, what would I do?

12. I am a spiritual being.

I must spend alone time focusing on self-understanding and self-love. To be present to those I work with and to learn from those I companion, I must appreciate the beauty of life and living. I must renew my spirit.

Appendices

Appendix A

Case Studies for Coaching at End of Life

Case #1: John

John is a 65-year-old man who has been feeling increasingly weak. After repeated trips to the doctor and numerous tests, a diagnosis was determined. The doctor met with John alone and informed him that his condition was terminal.

Knowing John has been ill, you pay him a visit in his home. He is now bedbound. As you talk with him, he informs you that the doctor told him that his condition was terminal. "BUT," he says, "please don't tell my wife. If she knew I was dying, it would be too much for her to handle."

On the way out, you meet John's wife in the kitchen. She asks if she may share something with you in confidence. "John is dying," she says, "but I don't want him to know. If he knew he was dying, he would stop fighting and give up all hope."

What are the key issues in this case?

Which supporting building blocks come in to play here?

How would you coach this couple?

What would your follow up look like?

Case #2: Mary

It is not your tradition to refer to a person as a saint, but Mary is the exception. Mary is a 39-year-old woman who has been an active part of your congregation for many years. She is a wonderful role model as a wife, mother and all-around Godly person. To your great shock, you receive word that Mary has been diagnosed with an inoperable brain tumor. You visit Mary in her home, where it is obvious that she is in severe pain. She is crying so hysterically that she can barely speak. Mary looks you straight in the eyes and manages to speak one word—"WHY?"

What are the key issues in this case?

Which supporting building blocks come in to play here?

How would you coach Mary?

What would your follow up look like?

Case #3: Jill

In making your three-month bereavement follow-up calls, you talk to Jill. Jill is an active, long time member of your church. She is 42 years old. Jill's husband Peter died suddenly and unexpectedly, while they were away on a family skiing trip. In asking how she is doing, Jill replies, "Not well! I was doing well before, but now I can't stop crying. I really need to get some help. I need to get over this."

Jill goes on to tell you how embarrassed she is at not being a better Christian example. This week when Jill shared her pain and tears at her women's Bible study, her friends expressed disappointment. They told her she needed to show more faith. With her crying all the time, she was not a good witness for the church or for Christ. After all, they said, the Bible tells us not to grieve.

What are the key issues in this case?

Which supporting building blocks come in to play here?

How would you coach Jill?

What would your follow up look like?

Case #4: Stacy

Stacy is a 30-year-old woman who is dying of cancer. She has no doubt that her eternal destiny is secure, and she is not afraid to die. Her pain is managed, and she receives numerous visitors per day. But the one thing Stacy cannot bear to think about is leaving her loving husband and her 9-year-old twins. Stacy tells you, "I am afraid my twins will forget me. I have so many hopes and dreams for them. I am their number one support. But they are too young. They will forget me and will never even know how much I love them."

What are the key issues in this case?

Which supporting building blocks come in to play here?

How would you coach Stacy?

What would your follow up look like?

Case #5: Perry

Perry is a 75-year-old man who is scared to death of dying! He is afraid of the pain he will experience during the process of death. He is scared of dying all alone. Most of all, Perry is scared of what will happen to him after he dies.

Perry has been a rebellious person all his life. "Wild living" are the best words to describe Perry's daily lifestyle. He alienated himself from every member of his family. He used and abused all of his "friends." Perry has never been interested in spiritual things. As a matter of fact, he ridiculed and laughed at anyone who got involved in such nonsense.

Now Perry is dying and is terrified. Being alone amplifies his fears. He is thinking about spiritual things now more than ever, and has no doubt what his impending encounter with God will be like.

His nurse calls and asks you to go talk with Perry. In his desperation, Perry agrees to talk with you. He opens up and shares all of his feelings and fears with you.

What are the key issues in this case?

Which supporting building blocks come in to play here?

How would you coach Perry?

What would your follow up look like?

Case #6: Pearl

Pearl was married to her husband Mark for 50 years. One year ago, Mark was diagnosed with cancer. After a hard-fought battle, Mark died just three weeks ago. Pearl misses him terribly and feels anger toward God. "How could God let him die? I prayed for his healing and my prayer was not answered." Pearl shares her feelings with her friends at church, but gets frustrated when they tell her that she should not be angry at God. She decides to stop coming to church for a time, but her friends tell her she should not do that. They say to her, "You must continue to come to church and be surrounded by the people who love you." Linda, Pearl's long-time church friend, says, "This is what sustained me when my husband died. I needed church and all the support I could get. So I will pick you up every Sunday. I will not let you stay away. You need to be here!" When Pearl persists in her desire to stop attending, Linda approaches you, asking you to talk with Pearl.

What are the key issues in this case?

Which supporting building blocks come in to play here?

How would you coach Pearl?

What would you say to Linda?

What would your follow up look like?

Case #7: Amy

You receive a phone call from Amy. Amy is a 40-year-old woman whose dad died eight months ago. She tells you she is calling about her mom. "She is a mess. She cries all the time. I don't know what to do with her. It has been eight months, and she still isn't over it! I don't know if I should talk about Daddy with her, or not even mention him. It seems like every time I do mention him, she just cries. I spend as much time as I can with Mom, but to be honest, the time with her is draining. What can I do to help her get better? Would it help for you to talk with her? Any advice you have would be greatly appreciated!"

What are the key issues in this case?

Which supporting building blocks come in to play here?

How would you coach Amy?

What would your follow up look like?

Case #8: Beth

You are sitting in your office with Beth, planning for the funeral of her mother, who died earlier this week. Beth's 6-year-old son Matt is also with her and is playing in the next room. After a while, Matt runs back into your office. You ask Matt to talk about his relationship with his grandmother. Beth stops you and sends Matt back out of your office.

Beth goes on to inform you that they have not told Matt about his grandmother's death. "We don't want to upset him," Beth says.

When asked whether Matt would attend the funeral, Beth says, "Absolutely not! That would not be proper. A six-year-old should not see a dead body. That would scar him for life. I love Matt too much to expose him to any of this. I want to protect my little boy."

Beth then looks you in the eyes and says, "Don't you agree?"

What are the key issues in this case?

Which supporting building blocks come in to play here?

How would you coach Beth?

What would your follow up look like?

Case #9: Scott

Scott calls you on the phone for a grief coaching session. "I'm a mess," he tells you. "I need help."

Scott's 35-year-old wife Amanda died suddenly two weeks ago. Scott has not yet gone back to work, and he cannot imagine when he will be ready to do so.

"May I be honest?" Scott asks you. "Of course," you reply.

"I think I am going crazy! I mean I think I have really lost it. One minute I am fine. I am smiling and doing some work around the house. The next minute, I am lying on the floor crying hysterically. Ten minutes later I find myself throwing things because I am feeling so angry. I am screaming at God, yelling 'How could you do this to me?' I haven't eaten for a week. I can't fall asleep, and when I do, I wake up a short time later in a panic, and then can't fall back asleep again. I have literally locked myself inside my house, and haven't left for days. I'm worried."

"Have I lost it? Am I going crazy? Can you help me?"

What are the key issues in this case?

Which supporting building blocks come in to play here?

How would you coach Scott?

What would your follow up look like?

Case #10: Richard

Richard is a 76-year-old man who is dying. He has multiple health issues, but the primary issue now is that his heart is giving out. Richard has been kept comfortable under the care of hospice and says he is prepared to die.

The hospice nurse informed Richard's wife that the time was getting close, and that the family might want to gather by his bedside. Richard is still awake and alert, but he is very weak. As the family begins to arrive, you receive a request to come support them.

With everyone gathered in the bedroom, all eyes are focused on you. The family is looking for direction. Finally one of the children speaks. "I feel like we should say something, but I don't have a clue what. Could you give us some direction here?"

What are the key issues in this case?

Which supporting building blocks come in to play here?

How would you coach Richard's family?

What would your follow up look like?

Case #11: Tina

Tina is sitting in your office in tears. Two months ago, her 16-year-old daughter committed suicide. It was a great shock to the whole family and to everyone who knew Tina. You have already spent extensive time with Tina, planning and conducting the funeral, giving support to the whole family, and talking with them about the grief process.

Today Tina is focused. Through her tears, she says to you, "I am feeling so guilty. I am her mother. I should have seen this coming. I knew she wasn't happy. If only I would have gotten her help. If only I would have stayed home that night and not gone to my women's Bible study. If I was a better mom, this never would have happened. I am to blame for my daughter's death. I could have done something about it, but I didn't. And why didn't I spend more time with her when I had the chance. I was so busy with my job, I barely spent any time with her. Now it's too late. I am a failure as a mother."

What are the key issues in this case?

Which supporting building blocks come in to play here?

How would you coach Tina?

What would your follow up look like?

Case #12: Pete

Pete is a faithful member of your grief support group. Most meetings, however, he sits quietly and listens, and doesn't share a word. After tonight's meeting, Pete asks if he may speak to you.

"I enjoy coming here," Pete tells you, "because I learn a lot by listening to what everyone else says. But I am not one to talk in a group. My doctor said it would be helpful for me to start seeing a grief counselor, one on one. I thought about asking if I could see you. But then I heard you say you were a coach, not a counselor. What is the difference between the two? Who do you think I need to see, and why?

What are the key issues in this case?

Which supporting building blocks come in to play here?

How would you coach Pete?

What would your follow up look like?

Appendix B

The Eight Building Blocks of Coaching

One of my favorite sections in any bookstore is the "how to" section. It's amazing how many "how to" books there are, and they cover an endless array of topics: how to build a deck, fix your car, knit, cook, find your perfect mate, etc.

This section is your coaching "how to." Over the next several pages you will discover the core competencies and skills of coaching—we call them building blocks. These building blocks will provide a framework for your coaching.

1) Deep Listening

All coaching begins with listening!

Don't read any further until you really, REALLY get this. It all begins with listening. Far too often we take listening for granted. How many times has someone tried to help you by offering you a solution, without hearing what the problem was? They mean well, but there aren't really helpful. Years ago, I had a medical doctor who would listen to me describe my symptoms for about 13 seconds, and then he would begin backing out the door, prescribing before I'd finished. I quickly learned the art of standing in the doorway.

So, coaching begins with listening—deep listening. The quality of our listening has a direct bearing on the quality of our coaching. We can't draw out the best in another person, or tap into their greatness, if we haven't listened for it.

Listening is one of the greatest gifts that you can offer another person. Listening, in and of itself, provides tremendous benefits. Consider the following case study:

Nancy Kline provided an opportunity for every member of a senior management team to listen and be listened to. The result reported was a time savings of 62%. This translated into 2,304 manager hours per year (Kline 1999, 70).

Another case study, Luke 19:1-10

In Luke 19:5-6, Jesus spent time alone with Zacchaeus. As a guest, Jesus would have spoken, as well as listened, to Zacchaeus. Based on the crowd's response to Jesus' actions

(Luke 19:7), it had been years since anyone had listened to Zacchaeus. The results were immediate and life-long. A changed life (Luke 19:9).

What is listening? Listening is …

- Being curious about the other person.
- Quieting your own mind chatter so that you can be fully present with another person.
- Creating a safe space for someone to explore.
- Conveying value. You are important to me!
- Not about giving answers, but exploring possibilities.
- Reflecting back, like a mirror, what you experienced from the person.
- Really getting another person.

And note that there's a huge difference between hearing and listening:

- Hearing is an auditory process. Listening is an intentional process.
- Hearing is done with the ears. Listening involves all of the senses and the total being.
- Hearing includes words, details and information. Listening adds deeper layers.
- Hearing is to know about someone. Listening is being with someone.
- Listening is a skill to be developed.

Coaches listen so closely that the answers almost come out on their own. The ideal listening ratio is to be listening 80% of the time and responding 20% of the time. Someone once told me that words comprise about 7% of what we communicate. In other words, most of our communication does not involve words. Coaches know this. That's why coaches listen at multiple levels. Here's a sampling of what a coach is listening for:

- Listen to what the other person is saying, as well as what they are not saying.
- Listen from deep within (gut-level listening).
- Listen to "get" the other person.
- Listen without judgment, criticism or agenda. You are creating a safe place for the person to share.
- Listen without thinking about what you will be saying next.
- Listen for values, frustrations, motivation and needs.

- Listen for the greatness in the person you are coaching.

- Listen for limiting beliefs and false assumptions. What does this person really believe the outcome or future will be?

- Listen for shoulds, oughts and musts. They are frequent indicators of obligation and guilt versus what the person really wants.

- Listen for the obvious. What is the other person not seeing or not aware of?

- Listen for the tone, pace, volume, inflection and frequently used words. Also, notice when these change.

- Listen for the larger context.

- Listen attentively to the end of the statements. Remember the old faucets with well water? You needed to let them run awhile before you got the good water. The best words often flow out last as well!

- Listen to your reactions as you listen.

To be able to listen at multiple levels, a coach must quiet their mind of any mind chatter or internal conversations. They must create a physical environment that promotes deep listening, by attending to the space and pace of life, and by managing their scheduling and calendar. Coaches grow to be comfortable with silence – resisting the urge to fill the space. As a new coach, I recall a seasoned coach saying that deep listening is similar to standing in a pool. In order to see the bottom clearly, you must be still—absolutely still.

Pause for a moment and consider your own potential barriers to deep listening. What are some steps you can take to address these challenges?

Here are some exercises to improve your listening:

Mute the TV. Since most of what we communicate is non-verbal, why not mute the TV and have some fun trying to guess what's being communicated? To really test your ability, tape the TV show, watch it with the sound muted, and then watch it again with the sound playing.

Mirroring. Pair up with a partner, with each person taking a turn to talk and to listen. When you're the listener, do your best to listen as if you were a mirror. Reflect back what you heard. Then ask: Did I get that right? Did I hear you correctly?

Tape record a conversation. With the permission of the other person, tape a conversation in which you intentionally attempted to listen deeply. Right after the conversation, write down what your deep listening revealed. Then, go back and listen to the recording of the conversation. What more did you hear? What had you missed?

Practice selective listening. Decide that, for the next week, you are going to be selective in your listening and really listen for one specific element. For example, you might choose to identify the values you hear underneath people's words. Or you might listen only for signs of frustration, or for signs of greatness. Over the course of the week, pay attention to that one select area, training yourself to listen for this one item. Notice when you hear the item clearly—what circumstances made that possible in you and around you? What was going on in the times when it was challenging to hear the item?

Remember, great listeners hear with their:

Ears. They listen to the spoken words, as well as tone, pace, pitch and inflection .They listen for the essence of what is being said.

Eyes. Most of our communication is non-verbal. Great listeners notice the body language of the one speaking.

Full body and being. Gifted listeners notice how they are receiving the message. They pay attention to what is happening inside of them as they listen.

2) Powerful Questioning

On my recent travels to deliver a coach training program, I heard a statement on the radio that stopped me cold: History changed when a single question changed; when we stopped asking, "How do we get to the water?" and started asking, "How do we get the water to us?"

What a radical shift for us as human beings!

My thoughts went immediately to how this relates to us in ministry. How would our churches change if we were to change our questions?

For example, here are some of the questions you might be asking now:

1. How do get "them" to come to us?

2. How much longer can we afford a full-time pastor?

3. How do we get people to fund our budget?

Boards and leaders literally spend hours on Question #1, but I think that if we changed that question, we could produce entirely different outcomes. What if we asked, "How can we go to them?" Or we could ask, "How can we have a positive impact on our community-at-large?"

Question #2 suggests scarcity thinking—focusing on what's lacking instead of what's abundant. What if we ask, "What more can we do with the resources we have?" What if we look at, "How can we develop the people we have so they can make a bigger contribution and everyone wins?"

In Question #3, it sounds like we're trying to cajole or even manipulate people into doing something they don't really want to do. What if we ask, "What are people most excited about, and how can we give them the opportunity to support us while fulfilling their own interests and passions?" People are happy to invest time, energy and resources when it is also satisfying to them.

I invite you to listen for the questions that you and your church are asking. Are they limiting, like our examples above, or are they powerful? And what's the difference?

One of a coach's greatest tools is powerful questions. Powerful questions are usually open-ended, leaving room for contemplation and reflection, instead of being limited to yes, no or specific choices. Powerful questions promote the exploration of new possibilities and stimulate creativity. They place the individual or group in a place of responsibility. They empower individuals and groups to consider what is right for them.

Powerful questions open us to possibilities beyond the reality that's in front of us today, stretching us into the territory of our visions to ask, "What is God's invitation for us in this situation today?"

Limiting questions, on the other hand, might not be questions at all. They may only be thinly masking a statement of blame or obligation of guilt, e.g., "Why did you do it that way?"

Have you downloaded the FREE e-book, T*he E3-Church: Empowered, Effective and Entrepreneurial Leadership That Will Keep Your Church Alive*? Each chapter contains 10 powerful questions that are guaranteed to shift your mind. Here are just a few samples:

- How could you make better use of the strengths of your church?

- What kind of leader would you be if you were driven by passion?

- What dream have you long since given up on?

- Which of your roles could someone else be doing, and probably better than you?

- What's the worst thing that could happen if you did less?

What makes a question powerful? Powerful questions are:

- **Directly connected to deep listening, enabling the coach to craft the most effective question.** Early on in my coaching, I believed there was only one right question. I would even equip myself with a long list of questions that I could scan while coaching. What I quickly discovered was that the most powerful questions were created in the moment, and the power of the question was directly related to my ability to listen deeply.

- **Brief.** They get right to the point. It can be difficult to resist adding an explanation or another question, instead of just waiting for the person to respond.

- **Free of any hidden agenda.** They are not leading or suggestive. In the coaching profession we refer to leading questions as "que-ggestions." Powerful questions help the person or group being coached to move further along the path of discovery.

- **Usually open-ended, promoting further conversation.** For the most part, yes/no questions usually result in a yes/no response, which force an end to the conversation and enable either/or thinking. Powerful questions promote both/and thinking, opening up the coachee up to a fuller range of possibilities.

- **Clarifying.** They help clarify and slow down automatic responses and thinking. Coaching clients have told me time and time again that they appreciate how coaching creates the opportunity for them to step aside—push the pause button—and discern what they really want.

- **Perspective-shifting.** Powerful questions invite us to walk across to the other side of the room and look at the same thing from a different angle or perspective.

- **For the benefit of the one we are coaching.** Remember that the coach is not the expert, and does not have to figure anything out or come up with solutions. Therefore, our questions must be designed to help the coachee discover and develop their own perspective and wisdom about the situation.

Types of powerful questions:

- Questions that help the person gain perspective and understanding:
    - What's the truth about this situation?
    - Who do you remind yourself of?
    - What keeps you up at night?
    - Is there anything else that would be important for me to know?

- Questions that evoke discovery:
    - What do you really, really want?
    - What's perfect about this?
    - What is the gift in this?
    - What additional information do you need?
    - How much is this costing you?
    - Who can help you with this?

- Questions that promote clarity and learning:
    - What if things are as bad as you say they are?
    - Where are you sabotaging yourself?
    - What's the cost of not changing?
    - What's next?
    - What's past this issue?

- Questions that call for action:
    - What's possible today?
    - How soon can you resolve this?
    - Who do you know that's going through this?

- What does success look like?
- What's the first step? When will you take this step?

The scriptures are a rich resource for powerful questions. For example, in Genesis 3:9, God asks the first powerful question of Adam and Eve saying, "Where are you?" Think about this. Why does an all-knowing God need to ask a question, when obviously God already knows the answer. Why then did God ask this question of Adam and Eve? The reason is just what we've been talking about: God asked Adam and Eve this powerful question for their own benefit, as well as for the benefit of the reader.

Here are some other powerful questions that God asks in the Old Testament:

- God asked Cain two questions in Genesis 4:6 and 9, "Why are you angry?" and "Where is Abel your brother?"
- God asks Moses, who is offering one excuse after another, "What is in your hand?" (Exodus 4:2).
- In the year that King Uzziah died God asks, "Whom shall I send?" and "Who will go for us?" (Isaiah 6:8).

Likewise, the New Testament also contains many powerful questions. As you read through the books of Matthew, Mark, Luke and John, you discover that Jesus was masterful in his use of questions. My all-time favorite question that Jesus asked is found in John 5:6. Jesus saw the paralyzed man waiting for the waters of the pool of Bethsada to stir, so that he could get in the healing waters first, and asks, "Do you want to get well?" What a great question! In the man's response, he blames others for not putting him into the pool. Jesus follows his powerful question with a direct statement, telling the man to get up and walk. And he does.

Here is a sample of other questions that Jesus asked:

- When the disciples were in a boat in a terrible storm, Jesus asked, "Why are you afraid?" (Matthew 8:26).
- He asked the disciples, when they were faced with feeding a crowd of over 5,000 people, "Where shall we buy bread for these people to eat?" (John 6:5).
- He asked the 12 disciples, when many of his other followers were abandoning him because of His message, "You do not want to leave too, do you?" (John 6:67).
- He asked the Pharisees, "Why do you want to kill me?" (John 7:19).

- He asked the woman caught in adultery, "Where are your accusers? Has no one condemned you?" (John 8:10).

- After teaching the crowds about how much God cares for them, He asked them, "Why do you worry about what you will eat and what you will wear?" (Matthew 6:31).

- He asked the man who was born blind—the one that Jesus had healed of his blind-ness—"Do you believe in the Son of Man?" (John 9:35).

- When Peter made his claim that he would die for Jesus, Jesus asked, "Will you really lay down your life for me?" (John 13:38). And then, after his resurrection, Jesus asked him, "Do you love me?" (John 21:17).

- When Pilate asked Jesus, "Are you the king of the Jews?" Jesus replied with a question: "Is that your own idea, or did others talk to you about me?" (John 18:34).

At the beginning of this section on powerful questions you read that history changed when a single question changed. And you've just read how our scriptures are filled with examples of how a single question dramatically changed lives. Questions are a powerful tool at our disposal. A powerful question, created out of deep listening, can change everything.

Below are exercises, strategies and examples to further develop your understanding and use of powerful questions:

Scenario #1: Your leadership team has been unable to take action on something decided months ago. Your team seems stuck on this issue. What powerful questions could you ask?

Scenario #2: You are designing a worship service and are looking for a specific response from the congregation. What powerful questions could you ask?

Scenario #3: You are meeting with a couple who is struggling with an issue in their relationship. They have a fairly healthy relationship but are stuck on this one issue. Each one is blaming the other saying things like, "She doesn't understand me," and "He never talks to me." What powerful questions could you ask this couple?

Val's Top 10 Questions:

1. On a scale of 1 to 10, how would you rate ...?
2. What's the payoff of not taking action?
3. What's the truth about this situation?
4. What's your vision?
5. What's past this?
6. What keeps getting in the way?
7. What's the simplest solution?
8. Who can help you with this?
9. What do you think about when you're lost in thought?
10. What do you really, REALLY want?

Some people collect stamps, coins or spoons—I collect questions. I'm positively intrigued by questions.

Jump start your next meeting with powerful questions.

A common complaint I hear from leaders is about poor discussion and input from team members: "How do we get people to share their ideas and comments at our meetings? We even send out the agenda ahead of time and no one seems prepared to discuss things."

Let me offer a simple change that often jumpstarts the discussion. Instead of creating an agenda with topics to discuss, develop a couple of questions from your original agenda that start people thinking. For example:

Original agenda:

1. Financial Update

2. Pastor's Report

3. Worship Team Items

4. Etc.

Revised agenda with questions:

1. What are some ways to encourage consistent giving over the summer months?

2. Who can help us discern the current state of our church and begin brainstorming God's unfolding vision for our church?

3. It's standing room only at our 9:00 a.m. and 11:00 a.m. services. What is our next step?

3) Artful Language

Many of us grew up hearing the statement, "Sticks and stones may break my bones, but words can never harm me." Nothing could be further from the truth!

Our words matter. Our language can provide a platform that propels someone closer to their hopes and dreams; at the same time, our language can reinforce doubts and limiting disbelief—dashing hopes and dreams. Think of language like a scalpel; in the hands of the skilful and altruistic, it can be invaluable, while in the hands of the reckless or malicious, it can have devastating or deadly effects. Language is like the paint brush in a coach's hand; it is the playground for our meaningful work.

Let's check out four pieces of equipment on the coach's playground:

1. Our actual words

2. The matching of words

3. Distinctions

4. Acknowledgment

Our Actual Words

Ask yourself—how are my chosen words resonating with the other person? In coaching, we often refer to this as how something "lands." Are my actual words fostering a safe and inviting environment that encourages the other person to go deeper below the surface to the core issues? Or, is the other person so busy dodging and ducking the zingers that you're hurling at them that they can only say "ouch!"

In our day-to-day conversations, words often contain assumptions, presuppositions, judgments, manipulation and suggestions. In coaching conversations, we intentionally choose words that are neutral, non-manipulative and free of any agenda. Our tone of voice is equally important. The same word with a different tone can be received entirely differently.

The Matching of Words and Language

Coaches notice the words and phrases of the other person. When appropriate, a coach will match their words and phrases with the person they are coaching, and introduce new words or phrases. Coaches also pay attention to the pace and pattern of the other person's language. For example, when asked a question, introverts tend to process first and then talk, while extroverts tend to process by talking. The seasoned coach will sometimes match the other person to convey a feeling of acceptance; other times, he or she will intentionally change up the pace and pattern to get the coachee's attention and make a point.

The coach is also listening for words that help the other person learn, describe their values and define their reality. These can be very useful in facilitating a shift. Often these are popular words or phrases from current or past culture. They can include TV, movies, music, metaphors, stories and quotes.

Examples of metaphors:

- The fruit doesn't fall far from the tree.
- Breaking the glass ceiling.
- Swimming in a sea of choices.
- Drinking from a firehose.
- Pulling yourself up by your bootstraps.
- It sounds like you're on a see-saw.
- It doesn't work to leap a 20-foot chasm in two 10-foot jumps (American proverb).

Examples of stories:

- Joseph's story in the Old Testament. "You meant it for evil. God meant it for good."

- The Emperor's New Clothes and the importance of truth-telling.

- Forrest Gump's "Life is like a box of chocolates."

- Humpty Dumpty's lesson, that some things in life can never be put back together again.

Examples of quotes:

- "And the day came when the risk to remain tight in a bud was more painful than the risk it took to blossom." —Anais Nin

- "It is a terrible thing to look over your shoulder when you are trying to lead—and find no one is there." —Franklin Delano Roosevelt

- "Most leaders don't need to learn what to do. They need to learn what to stop." —Peter Drucker

Examples from popular media culture include:

- The song "Don't Worry, be Happy."

- "You're fired!" from Donald Trump's TV show, *The Apprentice*.

- The TV show *Survivor* and the phrase "getting kicked off the island."

- A place "where everybody knows your name," as revered in the theme song of the long-running TV show *Cheers*.

Distinctions

Distinctions are two words or phrases that are close in meaning, yet convey subtle differences. Those subtle differences create a new awareness that is instrumental in propelling the individual forward.

- Consider the following distinction and the subtle, yet huge, shift it creates:

  Definition by obstacles versus definition by opportunities.

  - To define yourself by obstacles means that you are defining who you are and the decisions you make based on the challenges that you are facing. A life defined by obstacles is reactive. It is moving away from someone or something.

- To define yourself by opportunities means that you define who you are and base your decisions on your opportunities. It's not that you're ignoring the obstacles, you've just decided to keep your sights on the bigger picture—your vision. It is moving toward someone or something and is usually proactive.

Additional distinctions:

- Perfection versus excellence
- Adding more versus adding value
- Living by default versus living by design
- Working hard versus producing results
- Either/or versus both/and
- Prioritizing what's on your schedule versus scheduling your priorities
- Doing powerfully effective things versus being powerfully effective
- Planning versus preparing

If you've read our free e-book, *The E3-Church: Empowered, Effective and Entrepreneurial Leadership That Will Keep Your Church Alive,* note that distinctions are a much more subtle version of the huge mind shifts I ask you to make in that book. Below are the six shifts that I invite you, as a leader in your church, to make:

- From diagnosing to developing
- From doing to empowering
- From telling to exploring
- From mindlessness to mindfulness
- From excellence to effectiveness
- From professional to entrepreneur

Acknowledgment

Most people, when asked to create a list of their weaknesses and also a list of their strengths, find it easier to list their weakness. Why? Many people assume that "if I can just fix my weaknesses or if I could only correct what's wrong with me—eventually I will be great!"

Consider the following: The average person, on any given day, has between 12,000 and 50,000 thoughts per day. By the age of eight, most of those thoughts are negative thoughts (e.g., I'm not good enough. I can't do it. What's wrong with me?). Your church and, in fact, the entire world, are made up of people who already speak to themselves with judgment and disapproval.

Acknowledgment creates an environment of acceptance and safety. When people feel safe and accepted, they are more likely to be curious and explore new things.

The scriptures contain one acknowledgement after another from God to us. Consider the following:

- So God created humankind in his image, in the image of God he created them; male and female he created them … and God saw all that he had made, and it was very good (Genesis 1:27 and 31).

- For you created my inmost being; you knit me together in my mother's womb. I praise you because I am fearfully and wonderfully made; your works are wonderful, I know that full well (Psalm 139:14).

- Jesus acknowledges Peter. In John 1:42 Jesus looks at Simon (known to us as Peter) and acknowledges him by saying, "You will be called Cephas," which, when translated, is Peter—the Rock. Long before anyone saw evidence of rock-likeness in Peter, Jesus acknowledged what was there. This acknowledgement was a major turning point in Peter's life. Yes, the transformation of Peter into "Cephas" was a rocky one but it happened.

- There are different kinds of gifts, but the same spirit. There are different kinds of service, but the same Lord. There are different kinds of working, but the same God works in all of them in all men (1 Corinthians 12:4-6).

The book *Living Your Strengths* includes a Hasidic tale that teaches the importance of acknowledging our strengths.

When he was an old man, Rabbi Zusya said, "In the coming world, they will not ask me: 'Why were you not Moses?' They will ask me: 'Why were you not Zusya?'" That is God's question to each of us as well. We are not expected to be who we are not. We are expected to be who we are. (Winseman, et al, 2004, 10).

Ben Zander understands the importance of acknowledgment. In *The Art of Possibility,* a book he co-authored with his wife, he describes what he announces to every new class of students:

> Each student in this class will get an 'A' for this course. However, there is one requirement that you must fulfill to earn this grade: Sometime during the next two weeks, you must write me a letter dated next May, which begins with the words, "Dear Mr. Zander, I got my 'A' because ..." And in this letter you are to tell, in as much detail as you can, the story of what will have happened to you by next May that is in line with this extraordinary grade.

This practice acknowledges the greatness within people and invites them to live into that greatness.

Our God and our faith is about the giving an "A". It makes sense, then, that our churches also be about giving an "A"—genuinely tapping into people's greatness. Imagine if the average church in a local community gained the reputation of giving "A's", instead of judgment. Or, if the focus in a church shifted from who they are not to who they are, as well as who they are becoming. See your church as a place that is regularly telling people that they are fearfully and wonderfully made. How different would our world be?

P.S. In her book *Time to Think* (1999, pp 62-64), Nancy Kline tells us about how society teaches us that to be positive is to be naïve and vulnerable, whereas to be critical is to be informed, buttressed and sophisticated. Many people are taught that to be appreciated is a slippery slope towards gross immodesty. It is as if, when you hear something nice about yourself and don't reject it instantly, you will, presto, turn into an out-of-control egomaniac. This is ridiculous.

Actually, change takes place best in a large context of genuine praise, Kline asserts. Appreciation (what we are calling acknowledgement) is important, not because it feels good or is nice, but because it helps people to think for themselves on the cutting edge of an issue. We should aim for a 5:1 ratio of appreciation to criticism. Being appreciated increases your intelligence and helps you to think better.

4) Action and Accountability

When we began exploring action and accountability, a participant at a coach training event declared, "Finally, the good stuff!" When I asked what he meant, he said that everything we had discussed up until now, while helpful information, didn't really matter unless action happened. In many respects, he was right. One of the primary reasons that a person or a group decides to work with a coach is that they want to take action and reach their goals. Action and forward progress are indeed the good stuff.

There are three components to action and accountability: brainstorming, designing the action, and follow through.

Brainstorming

It's really tempting at this point in the coaching process to jump right in and design an action plan. I want you to resist that urge and instead take a few more moments to brainstorm. Why am I suggesting this? Our coachee's tendency is going to be to take similar action steps as before, if not the same exact actions. The trouble is that those same action steps are going to generate the same outcomes. The reason this person or group is in coaching is to get different results! A quote on my office wall reminds me of this principle: Nothing changes, if nothing changes.

Brainstorming helps someone see the same thing differently. Brainstorming enables the individual to discover different perspectives and possibilities for themselves. This involves distinguishing between fact and perception/interpretation, as well as gaining clarity and defining success.

A great example of brainstorming occurred during an episode of the TV sitcom *Seinfeld*, featuring Jerry's friend George Costanza. George was one of those people who couldn't do anything right. He was in his 30s, he still lived at home, he had no job or relationship, and he was losing the rest of his hair. And he was often thought of as being unattractive.

And then George Costanza had a major epiphany. George said something like this: "Jerry, it's very clear to me that my life is the opposite of everything I want it to be. From now on I'm going to do the opposite."

Do you remember what happened when George did the opposite? Things turned out very well because George was willing to look at things entirely differently and step out of his comfort zone.

I want those I coach to have those kinds of epiphanies when we brainstorm together before creating an action plan. I usually start by asking them to identify a next step, what they would usually do next. Then, I ask them to set that action aside for the moment and come up with 50 other possible actions. Most laugh at this request. Many are speechless. I re-state my request and give them some prompts, such as:

- What's the most outrageous step you could take?
- What's the simplest next step?
- Who could help you generate more ideas for next steps?
- What possibilities have you repeatedly dismissed?

Years ago I coached a pastor about casting the vision of his church. His usual method of vision-casting was to preach a rousing vision sermon the first Sunday of the New Year. Upon inquiry he acknowledged that this method stirred people for a couple of days, but produced no real progress. I then asked him to set that action step aside and I requested that, over the next two weeks, he identify 50 other ways to cast vision. He repeatedly stated that he didn't know any others. I repeatedly requested he come up with his list.

Two weeks later he came back with a list of 50 ways to catch the vision. Here's how he did it: The evening after our previous coaching session, he went to the praise team rehearsal. He kiddingly told the praise team about the outrageous request his coach had made of him—50 ways to cast our vision. The lead guitar player began playing the rock song "50 Ways to Leave Your Lover" and within minutes the vocalists began singing "50 Ways to Cast Our Vision." In the following moments, with the help of his praise team, he had his 50 ways to cast vision. Now he was ready to design the action plan!

Designing the Action by Creating a Plan

Within the context of brainstorming, a plan begins to emerge. The plan includes next steps that are attainable, measurable, specific and have target dates. In most cases, the plan addresses both what you need to do and who you need to become in order to reach your goal. Commitment, like the "50 ways to cast our vision," usually comes naturally and effortlessly.

Techniques useful for designing the action include:

- **Baby steps.** Sometimes people are immobilized with all that needs to happen. Breaking the action steps into smaller steps can help them begin taking action.
- **Backward planning.** Begin at the end (the goal) and then move backward and develop steps to get to the goal.

- **Acknowledging.** Recognizing what has been accomplished.

- **Creating structure.** Identifying what and who will keep the client focused on the task at hand.

- **Strategizing.** Considering what might derail progress and designing action steps in advance.

- **Anchoring.** Regularly reminding the person or group of the importance of what they are doing and where they are in the plan.

- **"Blitz Days."** Helping them carve out solid blocks of time to tackle everything that is getting in the way or needs to be done to stay on task.

- **Identify daily action.** These help create daily movement and momentum.

Sometimes formulas can be helpful. Consider the G.R.O.W. Model:

G	Goal	What's the goal?
R	(Current) Reality	How are we doing?
O	Opportunities	What are our current opportunities?
W	What	What's the next step?

Follow-Through

In an ongoing coaching relationship, there are built-in natural opportunities to check in regarding ongoing progress and to make course corrections. In most cases, I coach people twice a month—that's two times every month for us to follow through. I usually begin each coaching session with questions like these:

- What's happened since the last time we met?

- What didn't happen that you really intended to happen?

- What got in the way? What were the challenges?

- What will you report back to me the next time we meet regarding this action?

- What do you want to focus on today?

Notice that the accountability is palatable as we define completion. There is no judgment or shame involved. There is no guilt or manipulation. This ongoing accountability is a natural part of the coaching relationship. A pastor once stated that accountability is really about "goaltending."

5) The Coaching Relationship

In real estate, the three most important things are: location, location and location. It can also be stated that, in coaching, the three most important things are: relating, relating and relating. The coaching relationship is the vehicle of change and transformation.

One way to view the coaching relationship is as a dance. Let's use the example of that great dance couple, Fred Astaire and Ginger Rogers, to describe the dance of the coaching relationship. Consider Fred Astaire as the coachee and Ginger Rogers the coach. Notice that Ginger did everything Fred did (only backwards and in high heels!), but that she takes her lead from Fred.

Let's stay with the dance of coaching to further understand the unique and skilful way in which a coach relates. Fred and Ginger developed a safety and trust that let them draw close to each other. A level of intimacy was present, yet never violated. This allowed them to really "get" each other and almost anticipate each other's moves. Coaches are able to be totally spontaneous, while also being fully present and in the moment. This total spontaneity involves a knowing that is beyond what is typically, or rationally, known and observed. It's similar to the athlete who can anticipate where the ball will be thrown, before it's thrown.

New coaches often ask me, how do you further develop this coaching presence – your own deeper level of knowing? There are no shortcuts to develop a deeper level of knowing. It all begins with deep listening. Practice listening, and then practice again and again. Develop and use powerful questions, and make artful choices with your language. Here are some additional tools that have helped others I've trained:

- **Note-taking.** The act of writing helps many go deeper. Jot down what you're noticing in the coaching session. Remember, deep listening uses the eyes, as well as the ears. The challenge of note-taking is to take notes in such a way that it enhances, rather than interferes with, your deep listening.

- **Self-care.** It's hard to go deeper when you're barely managing life on the surface. Go for extreme self-care. It's time!

- **Review your coaching.** Make a recording of a coaching session and then review it. Then take it one step further and ask your mentor-coach to review it and give you feedback, specifically about your coaching presence.

- **Prayer and meditation.** Intentionally quiet yourself before and after a coaching session. How you show up matters.

- **Risk.** Share your hunches, inklings or gut feelings. Preface your hunch by saying something like, "I'd like to go out on a skinny branch for a moment with you, and I could be completely wrong, but here's what I'm wondering (or noticing)…"

- **Listen from the heart versus the head.** Be intentional in shifting from intellect to intuition. Request that the person you are coaching also get out of their head and listen from the heart. Ask them what are you feeling in your body right now? What might your body be trying to tell you?

Let's go back to Fred and Ginger for another unique component of the coaching relationship. Notice that Fred and Ginger aren't trying to correct or judge each other's steps while they dance. There is a mutual respect for the other's level of skills and competence. They each have their unique experience, strength and gifts. And the way that they relate to each other brings out the best in the other. On the dance floor they are tapped into each other's greatness.

How do you tap into the greatness of the other person or group? One resource to explore is my e-book, *The E3-Church: Empowered, Effective and Entrepreneurial Leadership That Will Keep Your Church Alive*, which has a chapter devoted to this shift from diagnosing to developing. In your day-to-day work and personal life, practice intentionally listening for greatness. At first you'll probably notice how much easier it is to diagnose, and how frequently you miss the greatness. Be kind to yourself—most of today's spiritual leaders, paid and unpaid, have been formally and informally trained to diagnose problems. Over time you'll begin to notice greatness more readily.

Next, begin to tell others about the greatness that you observe in them. They may dismiss it or disqualify it. Keep telling them anyway, because what's important is the shift you're making in how you relate to them—as a whole and complete person or team. Eventually, like Fred and Ginger, you'll be tapping into the greatness of others with ease and grace. And you'll also notice that your new way of relating will be an attractive magnet for drawing people to you and your coaching.

The complimentary coaching session is an ideal opportunity for a coach and a prospective coachee to discern whether you relate to each other well enough to develop a powerful coaching relationship. A positive coaching relationship will increase your coachee's likelihood of success. Since they relate well to you they are more likely to explore further and take bigger steps, plus they will stick with their plan of action longer.

6) The Coaching Agreement

As a pastor, I would often find myself needing to say, "If you need something from me, please tell me. If I don't know what you need or want, I can only guess at what you need and want. I am not a mind reader."

The same is true of coaches—we aren't mind readers, and that's why we have a coaching agreement. A coaching agreement is a way to define the requirements and process behind the coaching relationship.

The coaching agreement takes most of the guesswork out of coaching and makes it possible for the coach to follow the coachee—not the other way around.

While newer coaches see the coaching agreement as a once-and-done process, masterful coaches understand the ongoing nature of the coaching agreement, and that there are three parts to the coaching agreement:

1. The initial agreement
2. The ongoing agreement
3. The evaluation process

The initial coaching agreement includes:

- Defining the terms of the coaching relationship in writing; for example, fees, schedule, responsibilities and expectations of the coach and coachee.

- Articulating what coaching is and isn't.

- Discerning whether or not the coach and coachee are a good match.

- Clarifying the needs of the coachee and why they want to work with a coach. I like to ask, "What do you want to be able to say three months from now that you cannot say today?" This helps both the coach and coachee gain clarity about the desired outcome.

The ongoing coaching agreement includes:

- Helping the coachee clarify what they want to focus on in each particular coaching session, as well as what they want to take away,

- Further clarifying and exploring what the client is taking away from the coaching session, and

- Holding side-by-side the initial desired outcomes and goals that brought them to coaching and the current focus/take-away. Because coaching is focused on discovery and not outcomes, new insights and perspectives need to be continually integrated into the coaching agreement.

The third component of the coaching agreement is the evaluation process. This frequently includes course corrections, or may also involve a dramatic shift in the overall desired outcome. I frequently ask questions such as:

- How are we doing?

- Based on our coaching to date, what's your ongoing, developing vision?

- On a scale of 1-10, rate the overall progress you've made. What is needed to take it up several levels?

- What more do I need to know about you, your learning preferences or background to accelerate your progress?

- Where is self-sabotage showing up? What additional supports are needed?

- What will you report back to me the next time we meet?

A frequent mistake that new coaches make is in moving through the coaching agreement quickly—in as little as two to five minutes. I've discovered that the clearer the coachee and coach are with the agreement, the better the outcome. It's not unusual for me to spend the bulk of a coaching session on this area—15 to 20 minutes. Here are questions and statements that help my coachee and me fine-tune our coaching agreement and evaluate the coaching process:

- Tell me more. Because people are so busy, they rarely have time to think and talk. It's extremely beneficial to intentionally provide space for people to say more. Time and time again, I hear coachees extol the benefits of "getting things out."

- What is the one thing I need to hear in order to best coach you? This helps the coachee get laser-focused and selective about sharing only what's absolutely critical to their overall progress.

- Taking into account all that's on your plate right now, is this topic/issue the most important one (and if not, what is)? Similarly, this question helps the coachee hone in on the topics and issues that will contribute the most to their overall success and satisfaction.

This coaching scenario will help you to further understand the coaching agreement:

Steve is the founder and Senior Pastor of a rapidly growing church. He currently has 22 full-time employees on his ministry team. He frequently describes his team as a family. It's not unusual for Steve to "go the extra mile" and bend the rules for individual members of his team, because he considers them to be his family. He finds it difficult to fire even the worst of the ministry staff, because he's really concerned about their welfare.

Steve's vision is to grow from a single site to a multi-site ministry. He believes that he can do this within the next three to five years. In addition to implementing this multi-site vision, he would also like to spend less time at church and enjoy life more. His big dream is to take the whole year off and let the ministry run without him.

Steve has created a strategic plan and action steps to move towards his goal. He's making moderate progress. He is becoming very aware that his current ministry team is slowing things down. He is also frustrated that his "ministry family" doesn't share his enthusiasm for his vision. Steve initially hired a coach to help him implement the multi-site ministry plan, with a special emphasis on how he can empower and equip the ministry team to lead the implementation plan.

During a recent coaching session, Steve expressed frustration about his vision and his "ministry family," and then made the following statement about himself: "Maybe I'm the one that's holding back this vision. It feels like all the pieces are there, but maybe there's something that needs to change about me."

In your words, describe the focus of this coaching relationship (as may have been determined in the initial coaching agreement).

What are Steve's new discoveries? What other new discoveries do you see ahead for Steve?

In what ways will these new discoveries impact the coaching agreement?

In what ways will the coaching agreement remain the same?

After hearing Steve state, "Maybe I'm the one that's holding us back," how would you coach Steve?

7) Creating New Awareness

Brainstorming is an excellent way to explore new ways of doing things. Creating awareness takes it one step further and explores new ways of being, as well as doing. It's like working the plates deep within the earth, resulting in major shifts and changes. Let me give you several examples:

- Consider this statement from one pastor I coached: "I'm an introvert and everyone knows that introverts aren't good leaders." No amount of doing would result in any lasting change. This pastor needed to go down deep and create a new awareness of his strengths.

- Consider the leadership team that fizzled out partway through a visioning process. The consultant tried everything to get them moving, and then finally inquired about what was happening. After what seemed like an eternity of silence, one of the key leaders finally responded that they had gotten to this point on two previous occasions within the past five years and, in each instance, their pastor had moved on before the projects were completed. No sooner had the words been spoken when the leadership team had a major "a-ha." They embraced their new awareness and began moving forward.

- Consider the awareness that launched my career as a full-time coach. As a part-time coach, my business growth was slowed by the belief that I was just a pastor and no one would hire a pastor as their coach. When my coach helped me verbalize this limiting belief, it created an awareness of the truth that my ideal clients will seek me out and hire me precisely because I am a pastor.

Creating new awareness is like raising the blinds and letting in the light of additional information, perspective and intention. New awareness is fostered when:

- Curiosity is encouraged.

- Clarifying questions are raised.

- Beliefs and assumptions are articulated and verified.

- You intentionally consider a different perspective.

- You are open to other ways of viewing and interpreting the same situation.

How does the coach facilitate new awareness?

- **Contextual listening.** The coach considers and explores the various contexts of the person being coached (e.g., the bigger picture, the total person, previous experiences, the values of the person). When David pulled out his slingshot to fight Goliath, he was drawing on earlier contexts of time when he had fought wild animals with his slingshot.

- **Missing pieces.** The coach helps individuals and groups see and say what they can't quite see or say. Because the coach is listening on multiple levels, the coach hears underlying values, motivation, greatness, frustration, etc. Simply being a mirror and holding up for the other what we're observing creates new awareness.

- **Drilling down.** Similar to the layers of an onion, the coaching process peels away the layers and gets to the core issues.

- **Listening for clues.** A coachee is always offering clues about themselves. R.D. Lang wrote, "The range of what we think and do is limited by what we fail to notice. And because we fail to notice that we fail to notice, there is little we can do to change; until we notice how failing to notice shapes our thoughts and deed." Here are some powerful questions that will uncover important clues:

    - What kind of problems and crises do you keep attracting?

    - What do you keep doing that limits your success?

    - What thoughts are repeatedly playing in your head?

Eliminating Limiting Beliefs and False Assumptions

One of the most powerful ways of creating awareness in a coaching relationship is to help the coachee identify and transform their limiting beliefs and false assumptions.

Use the following list to see if you recognize some of your own:

- I have to have all the answers.
- I have no choice. I have no power.
- I cannot lead.
- Change is always difficult.
- It isn't possible.
- What doesn't kill you makes you stronger.
- Peace is always better than honesty.

List three of your limiting beliefs:

1.

2.

3.

List three of your false assumptions:

1.

2.

3.

Limiting beliefs and false assumptions can be very simple, yet very harmful. In her book *Time to Think* (1999), Nancy Kline offers a simple yet profound method of dealing with limiting beliefs and false assumptions. One of her tips is to help your coachee to articulate the "positive opposite" of their limiting belief or false assumption. This is often a difficult task for an individual or team to do, but press them to articulate the positive opposite of their bedrock assumption. Once articulated, ask them to write it down and say it several times.

8) Direct Communication

If you spend time with a seasoned coach, you will notice the masterful way that they communicate. For example, you will almost never hear a masterful coach ramble. Most seasoned coaches are clear, concise and laser-like with their words, offering one question or statement at a time.

Another characteristic is their comfort with silence. There is no attempt to idly fill space; rather, an appropriate use of silence and pauses is demonstrated. And coaches tell the truth. They don't hold back on whatever needs to be said, even if that isn't always the nicest thing to hear or the most comfortable thing to say.

Seasoned coaches are direct in their communication, using language that will have the greatest positive impact on the person being coached. Four of the most important direct communication techniques are:

- Interrupting
- Advising
- Directing
- Messaging

Interrupting

Most of us have experienced interruptions that are distracting or annoying, but effective interrupting is truly an art. As a coaching skill, masterful interrupting holds great benefit for the coachee, bringing them back on task, or helping them to "bottom-line" (get to the point).

Coaches interrupt within an environment of trust and intimacy, in which the coachee trusts the skill of the coach and knows that the coach has their best interest in mind. Interrupting can stem from deep listening, as a means of getting at something even deeper that needs to be said. Interrupting is a platform from which to catapult the coachee forward.

During my initial coaching sessions with new coachees, part of our initial agreement is for them to give me permission to interrupt them—when appropriate. Having this conversation on the front-end of the coaching experience helps the coachee to expect the interruptions and see it in a positive light.

When is it appropriate to interrupt someone you are coaching?

Here are several ways that I may interrupt someone while coaching:

- Say their name and ask for permission, e.g., "(Name), may I interrupt you?"

- Break in with "Let's push the pause button for a moment," or "I'd like to step in for a moment."

- Bottom-line it for them, e.g., "(Name), here's what I'm hearing ..."

Advising

One of the myths of coaching is that coaches never give advice. That's a myth? Let me explain. First and foremost, the coach wants to tap into the expertise of the one they are coaching. Got it! And, there are also times when the coach has expertise and experiences that can have a positive impact on the forward progress of the coachee. During a workshop at an International Coach Federation conference, the presenter stated that #7 on the top 10 list of what people want in a coach is advice. The qualifiers are that they want advice from their coach when appropriate and when asked for.

The problem with giving advice is that most people offer advice in ways that are disempowering of others. They need to unlearn how to give advice and then re-learn how to advise. I suggest that newer coaches completely refrain from offering advice, at least for a time. Once they have learned how to effectively coach without giving advice, they can begin incorporating advice-giving into their coaching when appropriate and when asked for.

Consider the following tips when offering advice:

- Listen deeply. Hear all that the person has to say.

- Don't offer advice until you have thought through how the advice may be misheard.

- Don't give advice until you have heard all the facts.

- Don't forget that it's ONLY ADVICE; it's not a cure for global warming.

- Phrasing examples:

  - Here's what I've seen work. Tell me if it sounds like it's worth experimenting with.

  - That's a tough one. Here's what I advised another person and this is what happened.

Directing

Directing is a technique for re-focusing or steering the person or group back toward their goals. This is useful for the coachee who frequently goes off on tangents or easily loses sight of the big picture.

Examples of directing:

- Hold that thought and let's talk about ...

- For the past several weeks we've been focusing on ABC, is it time to move on to XYZ?

- Congratulations. Let's move on.

Messaging

Messaging is a "truth" that, if heard, will help the other person to understand and act more quickly. It is a "blending" of acknowledging and tapping into the person's greatness.

Examples of messaging include:

- Tell them who they are. "You are someone who is ..."

- Endorse what they have accomplished. "Wow. Look what you've accomplished. Congratulations."

- Tell them what's next. "You probably need to start focusing on ABC, because you've moved past XYZ."

- Tell them what you want for them. "What I want for you is ..."

Appendix C

Supporting Building Blocks for Coaching the Dying

1. Provide a Safe Place

2. Be Present with Them

3. Invite Them to Tell Their Story

4. Discover Their Most Precious Possession

5. Help Them Share "The Five Things"

6. Assure Them with What Is Normal

7. Be the Student, Not the Expert

8. Encourage Them to Hold Onto Hope

Appendix D

Supporting Building Blocks for Coaching the Grieving

1. Provide a Safe Place

2. Ride the Roller Coaster with Them

3. Invite Them to Tell Their Story

4. Assure Them with What Is Normal

5. Give Them the Time That They Need

6. Be the Student, Not the Expert

7. Help Them Discover Their New Normal

8. Celebrate Their Growth

References

Byock, Ira, MD. *Dying Well.* New York: Riverhead Books, 1997.

Byock, Ira, MD, *The Four Things That Matter Most: A Book About Living.* New York: Free Press, 2004.

Five Wishes, http://www.agingwithdignity.com.

Hastings, J. Val. *The E3-Church: Empowered, Effective and Entrepreneurial Leadership that Will Keep Your Church Alive.* PDF Edition. 2010.

Hastings, J. Val. *The Next Great Awakening.* 2010.

"Hope in the family caregiver of terminally ill people." US National Library of Medicine, National Institute of Health, http://www.ncbi.nlm.nih.gov/pubmed/8496501. *J Adv Nurs.* 1993 Apr;18(4):538-48.

International Coach Federation. "Top Ten Indicators to Refer a Client to a Mental Health Professional," prepared by Meinke, Lynn F., MA, RN, CLC, CSLC. http://www.coachfederation.org. 2007.

Kessler, David. *The Needs of the Dying: A Guide for Bringing Hope, Comfort, and Love to Life's Final Chapter.* New York: Harper Collins, 2000.

Kinsella, Lois. "Walking the Hundred-Mile Road. A Parable for Someone Who's Nearing the End of Life." *Nursing* 31(3):62-3, 2001.

Kline, Nancy. *Time to Think: Listening to Ignite the Human Mind.* London: Cassell Illustrated, 1999.

Kubler-Ross, Elizabeth. *On Death and Dying.* London: Routledge, 1973.

New England Journal of Medicine, April 22, 2004, 350:17. http://www.NEJM.org.

NIV Pastor's Bible. Grand Rapids: Zondervan Publishing House, 2000.

Winesman, Albert L., Donald O. Clifton, and Curt Liesveld. *Living Your Strengths: Discover Your God-Given Talents and Inspire Your Community.* New York: Gallup Press, 2004.

Wolfelt, Alan D., MD. *Companioning You: A Soulful Guide to Caring for Yourself While You Care for the Dying and Bereaved.* http://www.centerforloss.com. Fort Collins, CO: Companion Press, 2012.

Wolfelt, Alan D. *Living in the Shadow of the Ghosts of Grief.* Fort Collins, CO: Companion Press, 2007.

Wolfelt, Alan D. *Understanding Your Grief.* Fort Collins, CO: Companion Press, 2003.

Wright, H. Norman. *Helping Those Who Hurt: Reaching Out to Your Friends in Need.* Bloomington, MN: Bethany House Publishers, 2006.

Zander, Rosamund Stone and Benjamin Zander. *The Art of Possibility.* Penguin Books, Ltd., London, England, 2000.

About the Authors

Dr. Don Eisenhauer is a pastor and a Professional Certified Coach, accredited by the International Coach Federation. He is the founder and president of Coaching at End of Life, LLC (www.coachingatendoflife.com), providing end-of-life training, resources, and coach certification. In addition to doing end of life coaching and leading grief support groups, Don serves as a Hospice Chaplain and Bereavement Coordinator. He is also on the faculty of Coaching4Clergy.

Other publications include the eBook *Life Lessons from Dragonflies: Helping us face the inevitable end of life issues* and the book *Coach Yourself Through Grief*. Don has a passion to help people live fully until they die, and to help equip pastors and other church leaders minister to the dying and the grieving. He is also the co-founder of the Bereavement Management Group, providing software to help in the care of the grieving. You can learn more about this program at www.bereavementmanagement.com.

J. Val Hastings, MCC, is the Founder and President of Coaching4Clergy, which provides specialized training for pastors, church leaders and coaches. Val hired his first coach while he was pastoring at a local United Methodist church. His progress was noticeable by all, and he began to wonder, "What if I adopted a coaching approach to ministry? What if the larger church adopted a coaching approach to ministry?" In that moment, a vision began to emerge—a global vision of Every Pastor, Ministry Staff and Church Leader a Coach.

Val is the author of the book *The Next Great Awakening: How to Empower God's People with a Coach Approach to Ministry* and the e-book *The E3-Church: Empowered, Effective and Entrepreneurial Leadership That Will Keep Your Church Alive*. Val currently holds the designation of Master Certified Coach through the International Coach Federation, its highest coaching designation.

Also by Dr. Don Eisenhauer, PCC

Coach Yourself Through Grief

If a loved one has died, then you know how painful grief can be. The emotions can be overwhelming. Many feel like they are "going crazy"! Nothing helps walking the journey of grief more than having someone by your side. But what if there is no one? What happens when you wake up in the middle of the night and wonder how to cope? What do you do when you hear your loved one's favorite song, and you break down and cry? How do you walk through your grief when, instead of walking with you, others want you to "get over it"? This is when you need to Coach Yourself Through Grief.

Read on to learn coaching principles that will help you during the tough times.

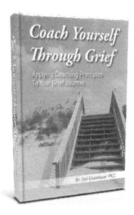

Available for purchase at www.coachingatendoflife.com.